EVERYTHING
IN ITS PLACE

EVERYTHING
IN ITS PLACE
STORAGE FOR STYLISH HOMES

Rebecca Winward

RYLAND PETERS & SMALL
LONDON • NEW YORK

Designer
Paul Tilby

Senior Commissioning Editor
Annabel Morgan

Production Controller
Gordana Simakovic

Picture Research
Christina Borsi

Art Director
Leslie Harrington

Editorial Director
Julia Charles

Publisher
Cindy Richards

First published in 2015 by

RYLAND PETERS & SMALL

20–21 Jockey's Fields
London WC1R 4BW

341 East 116th Street
New York NY 10029

www.rylandpeters.com

Text © Rebecca Winward
and Ryland Peters & Small 2015

Design and photographs
© Ryland Peters & Small 2015

ISBN: 978-1-84975-663-1

10 9 8 7 6 5 4 3 2 1

A CIP record for this book is available from
the British Library.

US Library of Congress Cataloging-in-
Publication data has been applied for.

Printed and bound in China

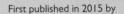

CONTENTS

INTRODUCTION

All too often, storage provision isn't considered early enough in the process of planning and decorating our homes – we're more likely to get carried away thinking about paint colours and the 'look' we want to give our personal spaces. But, tempting as it is to jump straight to the more glamorous elements of the décor, it really should be a case of first things first.

It pays to think about storage right at the start of planning a room; you'll find that both the success of the decorative scheme and your ease of living in the space are much improved. A home cluttered with so much 'stuff' that it can't be properly organized is chaotic and muddled, difficult to keep clean, and stressful to negotiate on a daily basis. Precious time is wasted when papers go astray and car keys disappear, things get damaged when they're stuffed into cupboards haphazardly, poorly ordered fridges lead to ingredients spoiling before they're used up, and crammed cupboards/closets can be prone to mildew and moth attack. And that's before you factor in the mind-calming influence of a tidy, well-organized living space.

There are two essential steps for achieving a perfect balance of practical and aesthetic considerations when sorting out your storage. Firstly, it's important to review your belongings and decide whether there's anything that you're only keeping for the sake of it, and which can therefore be jettisoned. Most of us tend to accumulate things that no longer suit our needs after a length of time – clothes that are now too big or small, equipment for hobbies we don't pursue any more, or kitchen gadgets that have seen next to no use. It's best to take a strong stance, and cull any objects that are taking up valuable space without earning their keep.

It's also a good idea to repeat this process periodically, so that you don't find that your belongings start to outgrow your home's storage provision. There are certain times in life that provide the opportunity for a clear-out – when moving in with a partner, moving house, redecorating or having building work done – and different life stages that have an impact on your home's storage

LEFT Once you've gone through all your possessions and discarded anything you no longer need or use, then the factors that will influence your choice of storage will be the shape and size of the rooms in your home, and the nature of what you need to store. Then you can start to decide whether your needs are best met by fitted cupboards, wall-hung shelves, under-bed boxes, or many other solutions besides.

OPPOSITE A streamlined look can be achieved by having a single statement piece of furniture custom built to suit the particular characteristics of a room, and also to meet the specific requirements of what you intend to keep in it. In a glass-walled living room, this sizeable wall unit is an essential practical addition. A similar approach could work just as well for spaces with a more traditional or classic aesthetic.

research its value by checking out sold items on online auctions, though for something unusual or valuable it's always wise to consult an expert. Second-hand or specialist antiques dealers, online or traditional auctions, car boot and garage sales and even selling groups on social media can all be effective ways to convert unwanted objects into hard cash.

Donation is also a good choice – either when the value of the item is not enough to justify the hassle involved in finding a buyer, or simply due to a lack of time. Charity shops/thrift stores will readily accept most unwanted items and there are also charitable schemes set up to collect large items – such as white goods and furniture – refurbish them, and then give or sell them at affordable prices to low-income families. If you don't even have time to look into all the options, you could always give away unwanted items via a freecycling forum, social media selling or a swapping group, or even through the small ads of the local paper.

Secondly, you need to organize your storage solutions to keep possessions in a way that suits the way you live. Think about how you use each space, and what needs to be kept in that particular area. The golden rule is to store items as closely as possible to the place where they are

needs. For example, first homes are usually small, necessitating some clever space-saving solutions; couples with young children often find they have a sudden accumulation of things that need a home; while parents whose grown-up children have moved out may still have to store some of their belongings.

Once you've decided upon what to discard in order to streamline your possessions, it should go without saying that only items damaged beyond repair should be thrown away – it's much more environmentally responsible to find unwanted things a new home. Before selling anything,

needed and keep frequently used items easily to hand. In the kitchen, for example, you might put coffee and tea canisters by the kettle, but store your food processor in a corner cupboard, while in the home office any correspondence that requires action should be kept in a prominent place, while historic financial records can be filed away in a less accessible spot.

It's usually best to identify the problem areas in your home and tackle those first. Perhaps you live in a property with a compact hallway, and keeping coats, shoes and bags tidy is your biggest challenge; maybe there's always a jumble of things abandoned on the kitchen table. By focusing on the most problematic areas, you'll make a more immediate positive impact on your experience of everyday life, so then moving on to sort out the storage in the rest of your property will not only seem more achievable, but more rewarding too.

Ultimately, a well-organized home is easier and more pleasurable to live in, so storage can certainly be seen as a central aspect to the happiness of its occupants – having a place for everything, and everything in its place really can be a life-enhancing step.

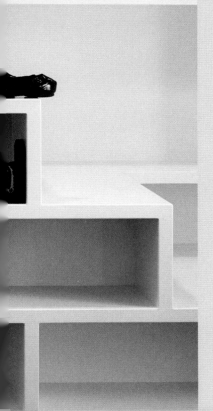

STORAGE BY ROOM

Aroom-by-room approach is particularly useful when it comes to sorting out storage. Not only does it help you to narrow down what should be kept in a particular space but it also breaks up the task into smaller chunks and minimizes the mayhem by confining the process (which inevitably creates mess in order to banish it) to one room at a time.

You might wonder where to begin, but the most important thing is to make a start. If you don't have much time or feel daunted by the challenge, pick a room that's relatively easy to straighten out — perhaps a bedroom or a bathroom. Alternatively, if there's a certain space that is really not working for you — maybe you are often tripping over shoes in the hallway or hunting through kitchen cabinets for equipment — tackle that place first. Remember that you don't need to go from chaos to perfection in one hit; you can take your time to achieve the order you're looking for.

In most living rooms, storage is needed primarily for electronic and electrical equipment, collections of books and other media, and comfort items such as cushions and throws.

OPPOSITE In a traditional living room, it's appropriate to have books displayed on open shelves – but you might want to hide away collections of **CDs** and **DVDs**, to achieve an authentic aesthetic.

ABOVE LEFT A chest can double as a storage space and a coffee table, and is perfect for stashing spare cushions and blankets, but make sure that you select one with a flat top.

ABOVE RIGHT This white-painted vintage dresser/hutch provides plenty of storage for plates, bowls, glasses and other serveware in a living room that also incorporates a dining area.

LIVING ROOMS

As a recreational space, the living room often has simpler storage requirements than the parts of the home with specific practical functions (for example, the kitchen), even though it tends to be the place where we spend most of our waking hours. The majority of living rooms only need storage provision for entertainment technology, media collections and comfort-related items such as firewood, cushions and throws. That said, living spaces with a dual purpose – those with a corner used for hobbies or a play area – demand special consideration (for advice on these spaces, see Storage by Purpose, pages 108–145).

LEFT AND BELOW A floor-to-ceiling stack of storage, featuring minimalist cupboard doors, provides plenty of capacity to hide all manner of things from view. Seeming like a blank wall, it recedes into the background, enhancing the feeling of space in a small room.

OPPOSITE This is a clever way to house a collection of media in a traditional living room. Minimalist-style fitted cupboards can work well in period spaces, since the sleek styling contrasts (rather than competes) with the interior detailing.

For an uncluttered look, try to invest in storage that keeps the TV, games consoles, media players and any disc collections out of sight – a specialist unit or a fitted cupboard will do the job nicely. If you don't mind your TV screen being always visible, there's no reason why you can't repurpose another kind of cabinet as an entertainment centre, simply by drilling holes in the back for the cables. Glass-fronted examples can be a benefit here, as remote controls will work without the doors having to be open, but make sure that there is adequate ventilation or you could find that your electrical equipment is overheating.

Coffee tables and occasional tables can also offer scope for storage. There are plenty of designs available with integrated

OPPOSITE Made with tongue-and-groove doors to suit the cottage aesthetic, this built-in cupboard offers a large low-level space that's ideal for storing heavy things – though it's also useful for blankets, books and board games.

RIGHT A pair of metal stacking bins makes a utilitarian side table. In contrast to the chest that doubles as a coffee table, their contents can be accessed without the top having to be cleared.

BELOW RIGHT Turned on its end, an old crate can be cunningly transformed into a side table – and it's just the right dimensions to keep a stack of magazines neatly in order.

shelves and drawers, and even some with a laptop table that rises up, simultaneously offering a higher-level surface and access to the storage space inside.

Alternatively, a chest or large storage box (or even a storage ottoman with a large tray placed on top) can make a brilliant substitute, but remember that the 'table' surface will need to be cleared every time you want access to the storage space.

Console tables and cabinet furniture on legs can be given additional storage provision by placing large storage boxes or baskets underneath (these are great for hiding clutter).

ABOVE In this open-plan living space, a recess – which steals some space from the adjoining bathroom – has been used to create a seat with built-in storage. Baskets and crates help to hide the clutter.

RIGHT **Wall-fixed modular shelving systems are a great way to make a customized storage unit. Simply choose shelves for display and cupboard components for keeping things out of sight.**

If you live in a period home, your living room may already feature fitted storage such as shelves and cupboards either side of the chimney breast. If it doesn't, this traditional arrangement is both pleasingly symmetrical and makes good use of the alcoves without encroaching too much on the floor space, so it is well worth emulating.

A more contemporary take would be to create a whole wall of storage, concealed behind sliding doors, where literally anything and everything could be stored, allowing you to have only carefully edited belongings on show in the rest of the space.

If your bedroom is used for more than sleeping, you will have additional storage considerations. Custom-built closets, dual-purpose furniture and under-bed storage are all excellent solutions.

OPPOSITE Following the principle of keeping things where they are most likely to be used, this built-in bed nook has lots of shelves for bedtime reading matter. The design of the platform also means that, should more storage space be needed, under-bed boxes could be used to store clothes or bed linen.

ABOVE LEFT When choosing furniture, remember to take account of its storage potential. Here, a vintage industrial trolley offers much more space for storage than a simple bedside table, while a bedhead that doubles as a shelf makes an extra space for keeping and displaying your belongings.

ABOVE RIGHT Rather than using boxes to store jewellery – which can result in items getting tangled up with each other – use a row of small wall-hung hooks to keep necklaces and bracelets tidy. This approach not only means your favourite pieces are easy to locate but also creates a decorative display.

BEDROOMS

If you follow the approach whereby items are kept where they're needed, there won't be much more to store in your bedroom than clothes. But if it's to offer a peaceful haven for a good night's sleep, a bedroom must be tidy and free of clutter — which means that adequate well-organized storage is of the utmost importance.

ABOVE Open shelves are superbly flexible, since they allow you to display cherished items as well as to store linens and accessories – though for the latter it's best to employ opaque, sleek-sided boxes in the same colour, to ensure that the look remains coherent.

RIGHT For the ultimate streamlined look – and a clever use of space – a bedside table and storage have been built into the wall. Made to match the wall panelling, the discreet cupboard door lets the decorative elements of the scheme come to the fore.

ABOVE RIGHT In a walk-in closet, open shelves and racks allow easy access to clothes and shoes. Keep like with like for an easy choice of outfit, and make sure that garments are neatly folded and are not too squashed in, so that they are always ready to wear.

OPPOSITE In a quirky take on built-in storage, several vintage suitcases have been given their own perfectly fitting shelves, so that they become a bespoke chest of drawers. Access is slightly difficult, however, so they should not be used to store things in daily use.

If you are following the practical approach whereby items are stored close to where they are needed, there will probably not be very much to store in your bedroom besides clothes and shoes (and if you are lucky enough to have a separate dressing room, you won't even have to think about what to do with those). However, if your bedroom is used for more than sleeping – perhaps doubling as a home office area or accommodating a large collection of books – then you'll have additional storage considerations (for advice on these, see Storage by Purpose, pages 108–145).

When it comes to clothes storage, many people like built-in wardrobes/ closets, which look understated and don't encroach on the floor space – a boon in modern homes, many of which have small rooms.

However, freestanding furniture is often favoured for its more traditional aesthetic and can be made to work well from a practical perspective, too, especially if you can position larger pieces in recesses either side of a chimney breast or in an alcove.

If space is tight but you prefer the freestanding look, make sure that you choose pieces carefully. Opt for bedside cabinets rather than tables or, even better, a small chest of drawers that is the perfect height

to use as a nightstand. Avoid the traditional type of dressing table (a knee-hole is a waste of storage potential) and choose a chest of drawers with a mirror fixed on top or hung on the wall just above it. In fact, making use of the wall space is essential in a smaller room; employ it also for hooks, shelves and cabinets, to store everything from jewellery and books to hats and make-up.

Whatever your preferred style, it is an excellent idea to invest in either a storage bed or, if you have a frame-type bed, under-bed boxes. The area under the bed is a wonderful place to keep bulky items that are not in constant use, such as winter coats and extra blankets. Also, while it is advisable to remove from your bedroom anything that has no good reason to be there (sports equipment or back issues of magazines, for example), a less easily accessible spot such as the area under the bed is a logical choice for the storage of cumbersome items if alternatives are limited due to lack of space elsewhere.

ABOVE **Vintage shop display cabinets can be a great choice for storing clothes for daily wear, as you can see what you need through the glass. In this room, louvred shutters protect clothes from exposure to bright light, which can cause their colours to fade.**

RIGHT **Adding an appealing rustic texture to a room, under-bed baskets can be used to keep your belongings neatly stacked under a traditional bed frame.**

While they're great for storing items such as books, baskets are not advisable for the storage of fabrics because of the dangers of snagging.

OPPOSITE **Where space is very tight, a storage bed is ideal, and those made with deep drawers in the base are the best option. The divan/box-spring type with sliding panels offers a bigger void, but access to its contents is harder.**

From foodstuffs and cookware to glasses, china and cleaning materials, in the kitchen a plethora of items must be kept ready to access or tucked away out of sight.

OPPOSITE In a small space, open shelves made of glass can help to keep the look light and airy. It's best to position them well away from the hob/stovetop so as to minimize the inevitable oily residue that occurs (this can also be reduced by powerful extraction), and to display only those items that are in regular use.

ABOVE LEFT Positioning a hanging rail adjacent to or above the hob/stovetop will enable you to store frequently used utensils close to hand so that they can be easily accessed while cooking. Do bear in mind that any implements hanging too low are likely to get spattered with grease or food.

ABOVE RIGHT Keeping like with like will ensure that you are more likely to find what you're looking for speedily. Here, a collection of baking ingredients, pastry brushes and measuring spoons has been given a home in a dish that can either be left on the worktop/countertop (if in constant use) or kept in a cupboard.

KITCHENS

Generally the busiest room in the house, the kitchen is truly multifunctional. We use it for cooking, of course, but often also for dining, socializing and doing the laundry, among other things, which means that it has to perform well when it comes to storage. From foodstuffs to detergents and saucepans to cocktail glasses (and including table linens, cookbooks, light bulbs, vitamin supplements, to-do lists and so on), there is a huge variety of items that either need to be kept readily accessible or hidden from sight.

So that meals can be prepared efficiently, storage for regularly used equipment and ingredients should be allocated close to the 'working triangle' – the zone demarcated by the sink, cooker and refrigerator. This will help to streamline the cooking process, saving time and effort. When planning kitchen storage, consider the type of cooking you do most often. If you bake a lot, for example, keep pans and mixing bowls close to your work area. Conversely, items that get only seasonal use – barbecue and

LEFT There is no rule that says you have to put doors on your kitchen cabinets, although the doorless look is probably best left to those who cook a lot and clean their kitchens rigorously. Larger pots can be used to contain smaller items.

ABOVE It makes sense to keep small appliances that are in regular use, such as kettles and toasters, out on the worktop/countertop, while supplies of coffee, tea and sugar can be kept there, too, if you like them to be easily available.

picnic equipment, or large serving dishes – can be stored towards the back of deep cupboards or on high shelves.

Keep cutlery/flatware, tableware and linens near the dining table, while the laundry basket and detergent belong close to the washing machine. Tea, coffee and sugar should be immediately accessible once you've flicked the switch on the kettle. Similarly, keep tea towels/dishcloths, aprons and oven gloves/mitts on a peg rack close to the cooker (though not too close, for safety's sake), cat or dog food in range of your pet's bowl, your favourite cookbooks within reach of your prep space, and recycling bins near the sink (or, failing that, close to the back door).

Store like with like, so that it is easier to find a particular item when

LEFT A custom-made batterie de cuisine allows pans/skillets, colanders and other cookware to be kept easily accessible.

THIS PICTURE With the addition of butcher's hooks, repurposed items such as this ladder can function well as pot racks.

OPPOSITE When it comes to storing heavy cookware such as cast-iron casseroles, it is a good idea to keep them stacked on a low shelf, for easier and safer access. If this shelf can be sited near to the cooker, all the better.

ABOVE In order to squeeze maximum storage potential out of a cupboard or wall space, position shelves as close as possible to each other – without packing them so tightly that it's difficult to remove items, of course.

you need it. Use containers and boxes to group things together in cupboards or drawers – clear plastic shoe boxes or large jars are great for this, since they are stackable and their contents can be easily seen. This is a particularly handy strategy for small things such as cake-decorating supplies or specialist ingredients.

There are plenty of other clever ways to ensure that your drawers and cupboards are well organized and that every inch of space is being used. If you don't have a hanging rack for your pans, use a pan stand or put them in a deep drawer and keep the lids stacked in a dedicated rack or behind a tension rod stretched

ABOVE Wire-mesh shelves, usually made from chromed steel, are both chic and versatile. If you simply add a few butcher's hooks to the shelves, you can hang pots, utensils and even ingredients from them.

RIGHT Store similar items in containers and put them on display. Here, a cooking pot holds utensils, a stack of tea towels/dishcloths is stored in a basket and everyday condiments sit on a tray by the cooker.

across the front of the drawer. It is possible to buy all kinds of freestanding racks and shelves that can help to increase the usable space inside cupboards, as well as drawer inserts that keep cutlery/flatware, utensils and other small items neatly segregated. Think creatively to achieve inexpensive storage solutions. A magazine file attached to the inside of a cupboard door is a handy receptacle for empty plastic bags or rolls of food wrap, or you can fix wire caddies to the back of a cupboard door using stick-on plastic hooks. Over-the-door

ABOVE LEFT Installing a floor-to-ceiling bank of minimalist kitchen units squeezes every inch of storage space out of a small room. In a larger open-plan room, it helps to create the feel of a 'living kitchen' by downplaying the functional aspects of the area.

ABOVE RIGHT Bespoke shelving or cabinetry comes into its own in an awkward or compact space. In this narrow kitchen, some shallow shelving provides larder-style storage for foodstuffs in matching jars.

OPPOSITE To preserve a sense of light and space in this small kitchen, wall cabinets have been dispensed with, so the base units have to work harder than usual. To maximize both capacity and ease of access, drawers rather than cupboards have been chosen.

clear-plastic shoe-holders can be pressed into service on the back of the pantry door to provide a home for all manner of small objects.

In a small kitchen, as much storage as possible should be wall mounted. Banish surface clutter by putting up a key rack, letter holder and noticeboard, and consider where it might be useful to site a small open shelf or a basket. There is often a strip of unused wall space between the countertop and the base of the wall cabinets, so think about installing a hanging-rail system to keep accessories and utensils tidy, a magnetic knife strip, or perhaps even pegboards to keep all your kitchen tools accessible in a gloriously utilitarian manner.

If you are remodelling your kitchen, it may be possible to make more significant changes to maximize storage space. There are numerous clever solutions to enable easier access to corner base units, including cabinet carousels and pull-out shelves. Drawers can also be fitted below base cabinets, in place of a standard plinth, while tall pull-out larder cupboards are great for squeezing maximum storage value out of a small strip of vertical space (and they are so much more useful than the ubiquitous built-in wine rack).

Storage space for towels, toiletries and cleaning products is a necessary feature of bathrooms. The best solution is to combine wall-mounted pieces with specially designed bathroom furniture.

OPPOSITE A grand, period room calls for a grand, period bathroom cabinet, though glass-fronted examples should reveal only a carefully edited selection of items. If you need to keep shampoo, conditioner and shower gel in plain view, consider decanting your favourite brands into vintage jars or bottles.

ABOVE LEFT Bathrooms usually occupy compact spaces. If this is true of your bathroom and you want maximum storage capacity, think vertically. This tall unit features both open shelves and drawers, allowing clutter to be kept at bay, while particular items can be put on display or made more accessible.

ABOVE RIGHT For a seamless minimalist look, and easier cleaning, avoid wire shelves and caddies in the shower and opt for a nook recessed into the wall. It should be just big enough for your daily showering essentials – any bigger and you'll be tempted to fill it with an unnecessary number of bottles.

BATHROOMS

Bathrooms can be spa-like sanctuaries or hardworking family spaces but they are always places for daily ablutions. Though bathroom storage is likely only to be required for towels, toiletries, cleaning products and medicines, it's still important to think very carefully about ease of access to allow for frequent and effective cleaning.

LEFT While a cabinet is essential in a bathroom, and especially useful if it is mirrored, items in daily use, such as soap and toothbrushes, are best stored in wall-hung holders or on shelves.

BELOW If you don't like modern fitted furniture, why not have a vintage table or cabinet transformed into a vanity unit? If the piece you choose doesn't offer cupboard space, storage boxes can be placed underneath.

OPPOSITE Fine antiques should not be kept in a humid environment, but if the space is well ventilated – and long hot showers are banned – you might be able to get away with having standard cabinet furniture in your bathroom.

An exception to the 'keep things where you use them' rule, clean towels should generally be stored with your linens rather than in the bathroom, as the moisture in the air could lead to problems with mildew and mustiness. For towels that are currently in use, make sure there are enough rails/bars for each one to be hung out properly – heated rails will help to dry wet towels more quickly, while hooks are to be avoided, if possible, since a bunched-up towel will dry slowly. Always include a ring or rail/bar close to the sink for a hand towel, too. If you are short of towel-drying space, you could consider attaching a rail/bar to the back of the door. If your bathroom doesn't have a heated towel rail, you can buy towel rails/bars that simply hook over a standard radiator.

OPPOSITE Wall-hung furniture not only provides ample storage capacity in a bathroom but also helps to create the illusion of extra space by maximizing the amount of visible floor area.

BELOW Lacquer, paint and wood are the materials most often associated with built-in vanity units, but mirrored glass is a good alternative. It is easy to clean and bounces plenty of light around – and it evokes a sense of glamour, too.

RIGHT In a pared-down yet traditional bathroom space, a large armoire offers all the storage space that could possibly be required. To help you to keep your belongings in good order, boxes and baskets can be placed on the shelves inside.

Most of your toiletries — except those in daily use, which should ideally be on a shelf within reach of the sink, shower or bathtub — are best kept in some kind of cabinet. This can be a bathroom-specific design, but you could also repurpose a piece intended for another part of the home. Many people mount their cabinet on the wall above the sink (especially if it's a mirrored design), but consider an alternative spot if that is more accessible. Fitted bathroom furniture is a great way to maximize a space's storage potential, and it can make cleaning more straightforward since it allows all but the essentials to be stored out of the way.

ABOVE In a quirky take on the wire caddies so often used as bathroom storage (usually chromed or perhaps even gold plated), a pair of metal baskets has been suspended from the ceiling on a chain.

LEFT Baskets can be very useful for keeping bits and pieces together – either on open shelves or in cupboards – but a caddy with a handle is even better for toiletries that are in daily use, since it can be easily moved across to the shower or bathtub.

OPPOSITE ABOVE The Uten.Silo II organizer, Dorothee Becker's iconic 1970 design, is ideal for the bathroom. Since it is made of plastic, it is easy to clean and capable of withstanding high humidity levels. Its differently sized containers can be used to store everything from razors to make-up.

OPPOSITE BELOW You can't have too many hooks in a bathroom. Although they shouldn't be used for drying wet towels (a rail or a towel warmer would be far better), they're good for hanging dressing gowns, clothes and accessories.

Vanity units with drawers offer easily accessible storage for small items, but, if you need to retain a taller space for things such as cleaning products and stacks of toilet paper, you can always place a plastic drawer unit inside a vanity cupboard to maximize its storage capacity. A lazy Susan can also be a handy addition, as it will make items at the back of the cupboard easier to access. If you have a pedestal sink, there are freestanding cabinets available that fit around the pedestal and provide additional cupboard space. Alternatively, you can find wraparound storage caddies, although these aren't quite as helpful when it comes to simplifying the cleaning process.

Wall-mounted solutions are a great way to beef up a bathroom's storage capacity. A shelf above the sink will

provide easy access to everyday items, as will a row of wall-mounted toothbrush mugs. A shelf above the door can be home to toiletries or toilet paper, while hooks and drawstring bags can hold anything from cotton wool to toe separators, and a suction-cup net or basket above the bathtub is ideal for draining and storing children's bath toys.

Whatever storage solutions you decide upon, make sure they can withstand humidity. Avoid fine antiques or any piece with a finish that could be damaged by the damp environment, and buy the best quality fittings you can afford – choose stainless steel or chromed brass over chromed mild steel, for example. It's also a good idea to fit a powerful extractor fan and make sure that it is set to the longest run-on possible, to keep the atmosphere as moisture-free as it can be.

When it comes to the dining room — or dining area, if your home has an open-plan layout — the question of storage usually revolves around tableware, cutlery/flatware, glassware and linens.

OPPOSITE Whether space is tight or you are just looking for a way to incorporate plenty of unobtrusive storage in an open-plan room, a built-in cupboard (perhaps with banquette seating) is a savvy choice – especially if it's painted the same colour as the walls.

ABOVE LEFT Open shelves provide easy access to china and glassware, so laying the table becomes a wonderfully simple task. If your tableware is on show like this, it's worth comparing different combinations of colours and shapes, as well as grouping similar items together.

ABOVE RIGHT There is no reason why you have to choose dining-room furniture to fulfil your dining-room storage needs. A sideboard or dresser/hutch might seem an obvious choice, but an armoire or linen press can offer a stylish and functional alternative.

DINING ROOMS

The chances are that you will be able to answer most, if not all, of your dining-room storage needs with one statement piece of furniture. Alternatively, you might opt for a custom-built unit with cupboards below and shelves above, or even simply wall-mounted open shelves to keep the floor space as free as possible. Built-in storage and wall-hung shelves are particularly useful in a narrow room because they can be made shallower than many floor-standing pieces. Another handy option for a small space is banquette seating with integrated storage (but don't keep anything in there that might be needed in the middle of a meal).

Storing breakables must be approached with caution. Plates, for example, should only ever be stacked in piles of eight or fewer, while avoid storing glasses standing upside-down (the pressure on their rims can cause them to shatter) or hanging delicate porcelain cups from hooks. In fact, if you have 'best' china that's used only a few times a year on special occasions, it could be worth investing in some specialist china containers and stashing them somewhere less accessible. Silver cutlery/flatware, too, should be given special treatment and stored in caddies lined with felt or in felt bags.

Another worthwhile addition to a dining area might be a wine rack, which will allow you to grab another bottle of red during dinner. If you are a keen white-wine drinker, consider a small chiller cabinet or keep an ice bucket nearby. Pursuing a similar line of thought, you might decide that the dining room is the best place for a drinks cabinet or trolley.

Finally, consider any other purpose that your dining room may have – perhaps it doubles as a study or a place to do homework – and dedicate a piece of storage furniture to that activity, so that anything relating to the room's additional function can be kept in one place.

ABOVE LEFT This classic mid-century sideboard offers shelf and drawer space for china and cutlery/flatware. The surface is ideal for display purposes.

ABOVE RIGHT A trolley is a good alternative to a drinks cabinet for those who love entertaining. Bottles and glasses can be conveniently transported on wheels to the desired location.

ABOVE Floor-to-ceiling cupboards help to keep this dining space free from clutter and provide a sleek (yet far from minimalist) backdrop for the boldly coloured chairs and rug.

ABOVE LEFT A vintage trolley has been used in lieu of a freestanding shelf unit – with the added bonus that it can be wheeled close to the table or out of the way, as required.

LEFT Glazed cabinets are a practical choice for the dining room, since tableware and glasses (as well as all manner of other things) can be displayed decoratively while being protected from gathering dust.

Hallways need to include storage for coats and shoes as well as all those small items essential to everyday living, such as keys, cash and outgoing mail.

OPPOSITE Putting up a few hooks close to the front door is a practical idea if you want to have coats and hats readily available as you leave home. Ideally, you should try to ensure that any garments and accessories 'on show' have an aesthetic that complements your hallway's style of décor.

ABOVE LEFT Shoes and boots can be hidden inside a storage bench, which also offers a place to perch while you're putting them on. This bench has become the perfect temporary home for a baby's carrycot – a bulky item that is difficult to store and needs to be kept in a place where it is easily accessible.

ABOVE RIGHT In this neutral, narrow hallway, a small collection of outerwear and accessories provides a splash of colour (as do the vibrant yellow hooks). In a small space, don't hang too many garments in plain view, and make sure that you keep one or two hooks free for guests' coats and hats.

HALLWAYS

The entrance hall can be one of the trickiest places in the home when it comes to planning storage, since space is often very limited. The key is to keep in the hall only items in regular use – so weed out any seasonally used belongings, such as rainwear or sports equipment, and find another spot for any shoes, coats and accessories that are kept for special occasions.

There are plenty of dedicated coat racks available, some that also feature shelves (and even mirrors, noticeboards or chalkboards), or you could simply fix a row of hooks to the wall. Make sure that you put up extra hooks, not just one for each member of the family. You could also hang tote bags on hooks to provide clutter-busting accessory storage. If you have children, include some hooks at a lower level. It's a good idea to give children a place to put their own shoes and school bag – perhaps a storage box on the floor, below their particular hook.

Sufficient footwear storage is a must. If your hallway is narrow, a slimline shoe cabinet is an ideal solution, or, if the space isn't so compact, a chest, antique settle or a wardrobe/armoire will keep the look streamlined. For muddy boots, consider a storage box with a plastic tray placed inside, or

ABOVE This is a simple country-style option for a small hallway. A rustic bench demarcates a place for shoes and boots to be kept (and provides both a temporary seat and a surface for storage boxes), while a row of pegs offers hanging space.

RIGHT Pleasingly utilitarian in style, a hanging rail offers plenty of capacity for coats and bags – so it's perfect for people who hold lots of parties – while shoes and boots could be placed neatly in the area defined by the piece's four feet.

THIS PAGE **A seat can be an important addition to your hallway, especially if you have small children or elderly family members – and, no matter how much provision you have already, it can't hurt to choose a bench or settle that incorporates storage space.**

THIS PAGE Be sure to check the dimensions you require before buying furniture. If this chest of drawers had been any narrower, it would have looked awkward (and its storage capacity would have been less); any wider and it would have seemed cramped; any taller and it would have interrupted the lovely sweep of the stairs.

HUSK!
♡ Garn
♡ Rosa träd
♡ Bånd
♡ Maling

invest in a boot rack. Repurposed furniture can also work well – perhaps a set of wooden pigeonholes for flat shoes and trainers. If you have an understairs or hall cupboard with a full-sized door, a hanging PVC shoe organizer will keep things in order.

The understairs area in a house has great potential, especially if you commission custom-built storage to maximize the use of space. The most useful kind involves a series of pull-out drawers that run the whole width of the staircase, and avoid the need for you to crawl through a waist-height cupboard door to find something at the back.

Don't forget to dedicate a spot to all those little things without which life can come to a grinding halt – car keys, money and important mail. While you wouldn't want to keep cash and keys within reach of (or visible from) the front door, you need them to be easy to grab as you leave. A small wall cabinet or perhaps a bowl or pot of some kind on a shelf or console table will conceal valuables while keeping them accessible.

RIGHT Wall-hung shelves and hooks are essential in a narrow hallway, where cabinet furniture might make the space appear even more restricted. It is also important to keep the floor area free from clutter. One solution is to use capacious baskets to keep shoes and accessories in order.

A hard-working home office can easily become cluttered or used as a dumping ground, but well-thought-out storage provision will prevent this from happening.

OPPOSITE A home office can be fitted into a tiny area, such as this mezzanine, provided you maintain a disciplined approach to organization and plan your storage options carefully. In fact, a compact space can aid efficiency, since you're never far away from the equipment or paperwork you require.

ABOVE LEFT Matching boxes and files can be used to create a streamlined, contemporary look – but if you prefer a more classic ambience, mixing various textures and shapes could achieve a more pleasing decorative effect. Here, a restricted palette of natural, black and off-white tones ensures coherence.

ABOVE RIGHT Whatever you use your home office for, and whatever your paperwork consists of, it is advisable to separate things by category or date, and label everything clearly. Small drawers can be particularly useful for filing, or you could use folders or boxes within larger drawers or cupboards.

HOME OFFICES

Whether you work from home, need a quiet spot for the children to do their homework or simply want a place where you can deal with correspondence and access the internet, a home office is an essential part of the modern living space. Such a functional area can easily become cluttered, and, if tucked away from more public spaces, there is a danger that it can turn into a junk pile. Combat this tendency with intelligent storage solutions and reclaim a clutter-free space that offers the perfect working environment.

ABOVE LEFT The industrial look not only makes a stylish option for the home office but also offers plenty of storage choice. From pieces that were once used in real offices – such as steel desks and filing cabinets – to pigeonhole units, factory trollies and lockers, there is a wealth of quirky furniture to choose from. You can also find plenty of new desk and cabinet designs based on original pieces.

ABOVE RIGHT When it comes to a paperwork archive, access is not as important as good labelling. Unless you are referring to particular files regularly, you won't remember which box contains historic bank statements and which is being used to store instruction manuals for household appliances. Since it is needed only occasionally, archived paperwork is a prime candidate for storage on higher-level shelves.

You are bound to have paperwork relating to home, family and work, and the home office is the logical place to store it. A well-ordered and clearly labelled archive of documents, from household bills to financial records, is best kept in hanging files; dedicated filing cabinets are quick and easy to use, though storage boxes that can accommodate hanging files can also be handy if space is tight. Alternatively, you could use box or magazine files, which can be neatly tucked away on high shelves if you don't need regular access to their contents. Buy more of these than you think you want, since your archive's needs will only grow as time goes by, and you'll achieve a more streamlined and coherent look with matching files and boxes. When it comes to storing certain papers, bear in mind that important documents such as birth certificates, house deeds and passports should be kept in a fire-rated, lockable filing cabinet or safe.

THIS PAGE The home office of a creative person will look very different from that of a home-based sales manager. Regardless of your desk's function, make sure that your most frequently needed items are within reach while you are seated.

THIS PAGE A white-on-white scheme with a sleek, minimalist approach – even if the style isn't ultra contemporary – will help to create an environment that is conducive to clear thinking. To avoid a bland and sterile aesthetic, use accents of black and chrome to add definition and interest.

At the opposite end of the spectrum, items in daily use – phone, computer, pens, diary – should be kept on or near the work area. It's a good idea to have an easily accessible system that helps you keep on top of everyday paperwork. A recycling bin will encourage you to weed out junk mail promptly, then you need a basket for unsorted papers waiting to go through the system and a labelled tray each for 'bills to pay', 'action required' (such as an invitation that needs an RSVP), 'keepsakes' (photographs, greetings cards and the like) and 'to file'. These will help you to keep paperwork under control and minimize the chances of your forgetting to do what needs to be done. Papers relating to current projects should also be kept handy, although perhaps not visibly – a desk with a file drawer can be a good option here.

The desk is a key piece of furniture and it generally pays to opt for a design with integrated

ABOVE To keep on top of your paperwork, it makes sense to work out some kind of tray system so that you know which correspondence still needs a reply, which bills need to be paid and which dates need to go into your diary. You don't have to settle for a stack of plastic office trays, however. In this case, a set of four good-looking baskets does the job admirably.

RIGHT Contemporary-style built-in pieces and period furniture come together in this home office. Its abundance of storage allows the surfaces to remain relatively clear and the decorative antiques to come to the fore visually. The two styles are linked by the use of a richly toned hardwood in the fitted desk, while cupboard doors painted the same colour as the walls keep the look light.

OPPOSITE If you need to put your home office in a room that has another purpose, it's a good idea to design it in such a way that it can be hidden from view – allowing you to enjoy the space without being reminded of work.

ABOVE LEFT If your admin needs are slight, a writing desk in the corner of the living room should suffice. Choose one with storage compartments so that paper, pens and maybe a laptop can be kept where they're likely to be needed.

ABOVE RIGHT An antique bureau offers the potential to create a self-contained home office within one piece of furniture that has a surprising amount of storage space – and it can be closed up when your work is done.

storage. If you like retro or vintage styles, track down a roll-top desk or a drop-front bureau, while more contemporary pieces inspired by the same principles can also be found. If space is at a premium, choose a wall-mounted table combined with (for maximum storage potential) a twin-slot shelving system that stretches from floor to ceiling along one entire wall. Alternatively, if budgetary considerations are a limiting factor, fashion your own desk by placing a stretch of old countertop over a pair of metal filing cabinets or drawers.

Once you've chosen a desk, look for ways to maximize its storage potential. Place small drawer units on top or stack up storage boxes to perform a similar function. A sliding shelf attached beneath the desktop will allow a printer and scanner to be kept out of the way. The wall behind a desk is a prime location for wall-mounted storage; it's a good place for small items that need to be accessible. A big noticeboard is a savvy choice, while pegboards, wall-mounted caddies and all manner of special racks and boards can make your wall space work harder.

A child's room needs to fulfil various different roles, from relaxing sleep space to reading corner to stimulating play zone. Practical storage will make tidying up a breeze at the end of a busy day.

OPPOSITE Nursery furniture may come with the option of additional storage in the form of matching under-bed boxes on casters – an excellent use of the otherwise 'dead' space under a cot/crib or toddler bed. Since they are also easy for children to access, they are great for storing toys, books and clothes.

ABOVE LEFT Any way of storing books so that their covers face the children as they're choosing what to read will help to inspire young bookworms. A wire rack works well; you can repurpose some picture ledges or wall-hung spice racks – or perhaps invest in a purpose-made children's sling bookcase.

ABOVE RIGHT Among the best places to store board books are boxes or crates on the floor. While this will allow the books to be accessed independently even by children who have not yet mastered the art of standing, you will probably find that every single volume needs tidying away each day!

CHILDREN'S ROOMS

If you are a parent, you will know how quickly children manage to accumulate more and more possessions as they get older. With the inevitable influx of belongings into the family home, it is important not only to get your storage solutions right but also to make the correct decisions when acquiring equipment – choosing compact, fold-down designs – and to edit possessions regularly as your children grow.

ABOVE In a shared room, giving each child a desk can help to ensure that homework is done properly. These three matching-yet-different work stations provide a place for stationery and favourite trinkets, while a trio of metal lockers offers space for books.

OPPOSITE Lower shelves or floor-standing toy boxes and crates are the best place for everyday toys to be kept, but delicate or cherished items, or equipment for activities that need adult supervision, should be kept on shelves fixed at a higher level.

Children may not need much toy storage in their bedrooms, but this depends on the size of the rooms, their ages and whether they have a separate play area (in fact, keeping play and sleeping areas apart can aid sleep). But aim to keep some toys in your children's rooms, even if it's only a few precious things that they might not want to share with boisterous playmates.

Beds that incorporate storage are useful for kids' rooms, which may be the smallest bedrooms in the house. Under-bed boxes on

THIS PAGE **This bespoke child's bed, complete with integral under-bed shelves that are ideal for toys or clothing, has been made to fit the space in a bank of built-in cupboards – but its casters mean that it can be moved to any location in the room.**

ABOVE School-style metal lockers offer a durable storage option for a child's room – and they would work just as well in a teen's space, too.

ABOVE RIGHT Painted furniture is always a good choice, since a fresh lick of paint will cover up damage caused by knocks and scribbles and also allow the piece to be updated as the child grows.

RIGHT This built-in bed with wooden shutters offers not only den-like privacy but also capacious storage compartments underneath the sleeping area.

casters offer easy access, while other options include beds with integrated drawers and cabin designs where a bunk boasts shelves, drawers or even a desk underneath. While it's possible to buy child-sized wardrobes/armoires and chests of drawers, bear in mind that these will need to be traded in when your child is ready for a more grown-up aesthetic. Instead, choose adult-sized pieces that are safe for little hands and lower in height but with normal proportions (and, for safety's sake, fix freestanding pieces to the wall).

Painted vintage furniture is great, since its look can be updated as children's tastes change, plus it's easier to justify customizing furniture when the furniture is inexpensive. Consider adding an extra rail in a wardrobe/armoire at a low height, for example, or fixing wooden spice racks to the side of a chest of drawers to hold anything from baby-changing supplies to picture books. Try to make it easy for your children to tidy their own clothes away. Think about the height of shelves and hanging rails, decide whether they can fold things up or use hangers and consider labelling storage boxes with photos of what's inside (underpants, socks, accessories). An easily opened (or even lidless) laundry hamper might encourage them to put their cast-offs inside, while a hook for the following day's outfit (chosen at the same time) may make the next morning's routine run more smoothly.

Go through your children's clothing regularly and evaluate it for fit and seasonality. A great way to store outgrown clothes and toys is to put them in well-labelled vacuum bags and keep them under the bed in a spare room or on a high shelf in a closet. However, to ensure they remain in good condition, avoid an unheated or damp space such as a loft or a basement.

LEFT A dedicated place for homework – as well as for creative pursuits such as drawing, painting and model-making – can be provided by a small child's bureau. Try to find one with enough drawers to hold all the art supplies and stationery that could possibly be required.

ABOVE LEFT A low but adult-sized vintage bookcase is ideal for repurposing as storage in a child's room. It keeps belongings within easy and safe reach, but is less likely to be declared 'babyish' after a time, in the same way that children's furniture ranges can be.

STORAGE BY TYPE

Most homes will boast a whole variety of different types of storage, from rows of hooks to custom-built closets and much more besides. It's a good idea to use a mixture of these types for the most complete approach to storage provision, but how do you choose which is most suitable for a given purpose? The key is to focus on the space and its attributes. Built-in, wall-hung, freestanding, repurposed, hidden and small storage solutions all have their particular benefits, making them better for some kinds of space and function than others. For example, wall-hung and built-in solutions might be the savviest choice when dealing with a small room, while freestanding furniture is often the way to go in a period-style interior and repurposed pieces evoke the right sort of feel in an eclectic or vintage-inspired room.

Capacious freestanding pieces such as armoires, chests and cabinets have a role to play in any home — not only do they make a style statement but they can hold a vast amount of 'stuff', too.

OPPOSITE If you have a large, open-plan space, sizeable storage pieces can be used to create different living zones. This will help to give even the biggest rooms a feeling of cosiness. Furniture originally intended for industrial or institutional use is ideal, since it has suitably grand proportions.

ABOVE LEFT Thanks to the wealth of designs available, freestanding storage pieces offer huge decorative potential. This chest of drawers, decorated with inlaid mother-of-pearl and fancy drawer knobs, provides such an eye-catching focal point that it's best displayed against a plain blue-grey backdrop.

ABOVE RIGHT Whether they are found in a fine antique or a veneered piece from the mid-20th century, the rich tones of natural wood will add a touch of luxury to a traditional sleeping space. Here, a large chest of drawers has been placed in an alcove, to ensure that the small room feels more spacious.

FREESTANDING

When most people think of storage furniture, it's the traditional large freestanding pieces that spring to mind first — chests of drawers, wardrobes/armoires, sideboards, bookshelves, desks and so on. Their familiarity might tempt you to shop for such furniture without as much consideration as other types of storage solutions, but a little forward planning will pay dividends in terms of both practicality and aesthetic merit.

LEFT Don't feel that you have to site a piece of furniture in the type of room for which it was originally intended. A traditional wardrobe/ armoire or linen press can work well in all sorts of spaces, from dining rooms to home offices, or even in kitchens.

THIS PICTURE In a child's room or hobby space, choose furniture that's robust and simple to clean. These cabinets are made from powder-coated steel, making them perfect for a playroom. Their low height gives easy access to the toys stored inside.

It's best to work out where you plan to put a particular piece of furniture, then search for an item that's got the right dimensions so that it will look like it's meant to be there. Beware of squeezing a piece in somewhere it only just fits, as the effect will be cramped – plus if you push furniture too tightly against the wall, it can restrict air flow, potentially causing problems with mould or mildew. Conversely, pieces that are too small can look mean, not to mention the fact you will be limiting yourself when it comes to storage capacity.

Don't be afraid to replace freestanding furniture when you move to a new house if the layout and proportions of your new abode are different to those of your previous home. Of course, if the pieces in question are heirlooms or otherwise

THIS PAGE Try to find furniture that's proportionate to the room. This large cabinet, which offers plenty of display space as well as a capacious cupboard, is the perfect size for this bathroom alcove.

OPPOSITE ABOVE LEFT For a coherent, calm look, paint furniture the same shade of white as a room's walls and architectural detailing. Junk-shop finds are perfect for this approach.

OPPOSITE ABOVE RIGHT Sometimes a single statement piece of storage furniture is enough. In a fairly minimalist space, this roomy veneered cabinet offers an abundance of storage.

OPPOSITE BELOW RIGHT A pair of matching wardrobes/armoires offers separate clothes storage for two people sharing a room. Keeping like with like should extend to the ownership of particular items.

cherished items, you might need to think more flexibly about which room they will suit, or perhaps even put them into long-term storage if you really can't make the space work.

It's also a good idea to think about how you will get your new purchase into its intended home, especially large pieces such as armoires and dressers/hutches. Measure doors and low ceilings, and consider any sharp turns, such as at the top of the staircase. Of course, modern flat-pack options are unlikely to be any sort of problem, but if you're buying craftsman-made furniture or antiques, then it's an essential consideration. You might like to investigate whether bespoke pieces can be put together in situ if access is restricted, or maybe opt for an antique that was originally designed to be taken apart for re-siting (such as campaign furniture, or a knock-down wardrobe/armoire).

Especially designed to suit your home, possessions and lifestyle, this type of storage works hard and looks great. If you're refurbishing or building from scratch, plan for plenty of custom-built storage.

OPPOSITE Why go to the trouble of finding a dresser/hutch to fit an alcove exactly, when you can have the fitted equivalent custom-made? This approach has the added benefit that there are no awkward corners where dust can gather, so it won't be necessary to move heavy furniture in order to clean the room.

ABOVE LEFT A floor-to-ceiling run of kitchen cabinets can offer a huge amount of storage while looking sleek and streamlined. It's an approach that works whether your chosen aesthetic is modern minimalism or classic farmhouse. Here, an in-frame design evokes a sense of traditional charm.

ABOVE RIGHT One of the best things about custom-built storage is that you can dictate every aspect of the design, from colour and style to dimensions and design features (so the items to be stored can be perfectly accommodated). Some craftspeople are happy to work with reclaimed materials, for a vintage vibe.

CUSTOM-BUILT

What's not to love about custom-built storage? Made-to-measure built-in storage solutions not only maximize the storage potential of even the most awkward or tiny spaces but they're the perfect way to streamline a room's look, too.

In a small room, cleverly designed custom-built storage really comes into its own, thanks to its clutter-concealing abilities. A floor-to-ceiling built-in design maximizes storage in relation to the footprint of the interior, so by shaving off even a relatively small strip of floor area, it is possible to achieve significant storage provision without making a room seem cramped or busy.

LEFT Featuring flat doors that are all identical in size, this wall of built-in cupboards is the perfect choice for a minimalist space – both in terms of style and the potential for all possessions to be hidden from view.

ABOVE An original built-in cupboard has been teamed with simple shelves, painted to match the wall, to create an installation resembling a dresser/ hutch that is modern and authentic at the same time.

OPPOSITE Wonderful for squeezing maximum storage potential from every inch of space, bespoke cupboards are ideal for rooms with sloping ceilings – and the resulting look is also more streamlined and coherent.

THIS PAGE **When designing bespoke fitted furniture, there is plenty of scope for meeting your storage needs in an imaginative way. This built-in bench includes capacious under-seat drawers that are great for hiding things away – meaning that only possessions with aesthetic appeal need be out on display.**

At the opposite end of the floor-space spectrum, made-to-measure storage can be the ideal solution for demarcating different zones within a large, open-plan area. For example, a relaxing sitting area might be cosily screened off from a kitchen-diner with a full-height room divider, or an elegant dining area can be kept distinct from the working part of a kitchen with a counter-height unit.

If a room is built in the eaves of the roof or has an alcove, or you're looking to make the most of under-stairs space, then custom-built storage is likely to be your best bet. Similarly, if an area is too small or narrow to allow for standard freestanding pieces, then some kind of bespoke wall-fixed cabinet might be called for, or maybe a solution such as banquette seating with integrated storage space or a built-in bed with integrated drawers.

ABOVE RIGHT A tailor-made approach has been taken to this reading nook, with the result that it is entirely suited to its purpose. The inclusion of a comfortable seat, several drawers and plenty of room for favourite novels on the shelves above makes a small space work hard.

RIGHT Since these fitted cupboard do not extend right up to the ceiling, the room retains a more traditional feel. This feature also helps to avoid making a tall space appear even taller – as well as offering decorative display potential.

All homes will benefit from practical and versatile wall-hung storage. Shelves are the most commonly thought-of example of this type of storage, although a wide variety of choices is available.

OPPOSITE There can never be too many hooks in a hallway, and it is a sensible idea to have one or two spare for guests to use. But there is no rule that says the hooks have to match — indeed, a collection of similarly scaled yet differently shaped hooks can create an attractive decorative effect.

ABOVE LEFT Wall-hung storage cannot be beaten when it comes to maximizing the space in a small room – and it's wonderful for maintaining a feeling of openness, too. Look for pieces that are multifunctional, such as this bedside cabinet with a drop front, which can also be used as a desk or a table.

ABOVE RIGHT A wall-hung shelf unit is perfect in a kitchen. As well as holding glasses and other everyday things (which are fine on open shelves, since there's no time for them to gather dust), it's good for storing items that might otherwise clutter up the worktop/countertop, such as pencils and bunches of keys.

WALL-HUNG

Nothing is more useful in small spaces than wall-hung storage, since it keeps the floor area free, which is a benefit from both a practical and aesthetic perspective. It is, however, best to position wall-hung pieces carefully, especially in areas that are throughways or otherwise potentially hazardous. Don't hang shelves above a cot/crib or child's bed, for example, and take care that hooks and pegs don't project too far into a narrow hallway.

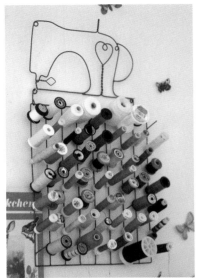

Shelves may immediately spring to mind as a wall-hung storage solution, but there are many different options to choose from, ranging from single hooks to large customizable wall-mounted storage systems that are intended for use in the workroom, garage or walk-in wardrobe/closet.

Rows of hooks or pegs (especially those with a narrow shelf above) are useful in pretty much every part of the home, whether for coats and hats near the front door or robes in the bathroom. They're a great choice for spare bedrooms as well, offering somewhere for guests to hang their clothes if there's little or no cupboard space available. Wall cabinets also have the benefit of hiding things away (for example, toiletries in the bathroom), or if glass-fronted they

OPPOSITE LEFT Floating shelves are the ultimate in minimalist wall-hung storage. Make sure that they are firmly fixed, and don't overload them, since they are not as strong as designs with supporting brackets.

OPPOSITE RIGHT Open wall-hung storage is ideal in any space that has a specific purpose, such as a sewing room. Tailor-made solutions, such as this spool rack, make it possible to keep equipment close at hand.

THIS PAGE A front-facing plate rack can work decoratively as well as practically. This collection of differently shaped platters would have been difficult to store safely in a stack.

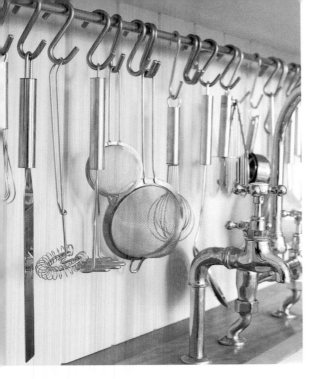

ABOVE LEFT **Installing a rail and some butcher's hooks above the worktop/countertop not only makes the most of often under-used wall space but also ensures that your cooking utensils are always within easy reach.**

ABOVE RIGHT **Wall-hung systems that allow you to create your own configuration of hooks, shelves and stemware-holders are tremendously useful, since you can customize them to suit your needs exactly.**

OPPOSITE **If space is extra-tight in the kitchen, a plate rack with integrated shelving might accommodate all your everyday cookware and china. Some plate racks feature drainage holes in the bottom so that dishes can drip dry.**

can both store and display a cherished collection (china, glassware or even favourite shoes). Don't feel you are limited to purpose-designed wall cabinets – small floor-standing designs can be wall mounted with the right fixings, while repurposed items can be used as cabinets, too, for example boxes or tins with hinged lids.

There are also numerous types of wall-hung storage with a specific purpose, such as magazine holders, plate racks, bicycle hooks and utensil rails. It's worth being open-minded about their purpose, as some can function beautifully for other types of object. For instance, spice racks work brilliantly as children's book shelves, while a magnetic knife strip intended for kitchen use can also

function as a storage solution for lightweight metal items elsewhere, perhaps in the bathroom (for hair grips and tweezers) or the hobby room (for small tools).

Whatever wall-hung storage you opt for, choose your design and wall fixings to suit the weight of the items you intend to store. For example, 'floating' shelves should be used for lighter items rather than heavy books, since their concealed fixings can't bear a great deal of weight – for anything substantial, it's far better to use a shelf with brackets so that the load is spread over a greater area. You'll need to find out the construction of your walls, too (solid masonry or stud with plasterboard), in order to select suitable wallplugs for the job.

Sleek and streamlined, clever hidden storage conceals mess and clutter. Custom-built examples may require forward planning, but there are also pieces of furniture that can play a dual role.

OPPOSITE This hallway is also a laundry room and linen store – but you'd never know it unless you opened the doors. As well as a cupboard for clean towels and sheets, there are laundry bins inside the built-in bench, and on the other side of the room there's a washing machine behind a matching cupboard door.

ABOVE LEFT A studio or pied à terre will require some some nifty creative thinking when it comes to making the most of the available space. In this tiny apartment, a small door offers access to the space underneath a mezzanine level. The door has been painted the same shade as the wall to blend in seamlessly.

ABOVE RIGHT A perfect example of making the most of any available space, the discreet door in the wall shown above left swings open to reveal a front-loading washing machine. An awkward nook under the stairs or below low eaves could provide a home for a washing machine and/or a dryer.

CONCEALED

A lot of storage options work to hide away various items – clutter-free, streamlined interiors simply aren't achievable without either suitable storage or a spartan approach to personal belongings – but there are some ingenious solutions that are themselves hidden.

Custom-built designs offer plenty of potential for clever hidden storage – banquette seating, drawers integrated into beds and staircases, sliding coat racks under the stairs, or even wooden bathtub panels on hinges that open out to reveal space for cleaning products, are all the sort of schemes that it's possible to create with a little ingenuity and some carpentry skills (or the assistance of a competent professional). More ambitiously, it's also possible to create concealed kitchens (which look just like a sleek wall of cupboards until required), spiral wine cellars sunk into the floor, and, if you have the space and the need, even completely hidden 'secret' rooms.

There might also be some small objects of high or sentimental value that you would prefer to store safely out of sight, and there are some less elaborate custom-made solutions that could fulfil this need. A jewellery board can be fitted behind a swing-out mirror, recessed shelves (or even a mini safe) may be inserted into the wall (behind a mirror or picture) in the hallway for car keys and cash, while a storage headboard with hinged upholstered panels could be another safe place for cherished keepsakes.

OPPOSITE LEFT Accommodating a library-sized collection of books is not particularly compatible with the minimalist aesthetic, but this ingenious hidden bookcase makes it possible to achieve the latter without having to compromise on the former.

OPPOSITE RIGHT Were it not for the subtle cut-out handles on this storage window seat, painted white to match the walls for maximum subtlety, you'd never know there was a large cupboard lurking beneath its cushioned surface.

RIGHT These open shelves are currently being used for display purposes, but thanks to the presence of a floor-to-ceiling curtain, less attractive pieces can successfully be hidden from view.

But if all that sounds like it's more work or expense than you're willing to take on, there are also numerous pieces of furniture that cleverly contain hidden integrated storage. Hinge-topped or lidded ottomans, whether antique or from Ikea, are always a practical choice in the living room or bedroom, for example. It's also possible to track down sofas and beds that contain capacious storage compartments (the seat or mattress is hinged, so it easily lifts up to reveal a storage space below). Other options worth exploring are smaller, more traditional pieces such as piano stools, hall settles and benches, upholstered foot stools and storage coffee tables.

Alternatively, if you are looking for a quick and easy DIY clutter-busting solution and your sewing skills are up to scratch, why not make a fabric slipcover to cover a side table or a simple gathered curtain to fit around the legs of a console table or to cover a set of shelves, and conceal storage baskets or boxes behind the swathe of fabric?

Bring calm and order to any busy space by investing in a selection of smaller storage items. Boxes, crates, files and tins will beat clutter and provide a home for everything, no matter how small.

OPPOSITE Desk-top shelf units or mini pigeonhole units – which are handy for displaying decorative pieces as well as for practical things – will help you to keep everything you need around you when you are working. A noticeboard is another useful addition, whether it's used for paperwork or inspiring imagery.

ABOVE LEFT Storage boxes divided into compartments are perfect for keeping hobby supplies tidy, and there's lots of scope for creating eye-catching little vignettes, too. The sections in this wooden box have been lined with green and pink paper, which matches the colours of the container's contents.

ABOVE RIGHT You don't need to buy purpose-made storage boxes. Keep your eyes open for attractive, well-made packaging or vintage tins. You could even cover plain boxes with patterned paper (or just personalize them with washi tape) for a stylish and unique solution to the challenge of storing small items.

SMALL-SCALE

Small-scale storage is often known as secondary storage, as it's generally used to keep things in order within, below or on top of other furniture. From repurposed food packaging to purpose-made compartmentalized caddies, there's a wealth of options out there – it's just a case of choosing the right ones to suit your style and purpose.

Storage boxes with lids are ideal for creating a streamlined clutter-free look, as well as keeping objects safely together and dust-free. Whether you line them along shelves, tuck them under console tables or place them atop a wardrobe/armoire, they're an affordable, versatile solution, available in all shapes and sizes. Of course, you don't necessarily need to buy this sort of thing specifically, as you can repurpose all manner of packaging to perform the same function, giving new life to hat boxes, cookie tins, glass food jars and the like.

Baskets and hampers offer country charm, but they need a fabric liner to protect delicate items from being snagged, plus their open weave doesn't protect against dust. Crates and wire baskets can offer a similar solution, though one with a more industrial edge (the former are particularly good candidates for having casters attached, for ease of movement). Open-topped jugs/pitchers and pots of various kinds are useful for storing utensils in the kitchen, pens and pencils in the home office and toothbrushes in the bathroom. In fact, any small receptacle can be pressed into use where tiny items need to

ABOVE LEFT For a streamlined look, matching storage boxes lined up on a shelf are hard to beat. In this case, white boxes fill the white shelf unit compartments almost exactly, giving a pleasingly harmonious effect (not to mention maximum storage capacity).

ABOVE RIGHT Creative thinking can help you to find storage capacity in unexpected places. The shape of this stool allows a stack of magazines to be slotted between its legs, while the flat top acts as a side table.

OPPOSITE You can economize on small storage by repurposing existing objects. Wooden crates – whether covered with paper or fabric, painted or left natural – can be stacked up to form a shelf-like arrangement, with jam jars and old tins serving as containers.

THIS PAGE A wooden box set on its side demarcates a storage area for bowls and pans, as well as providing a shelf for utensils and ingredients. A couple of hooks offer scope for hanging more kitchen paraphernalia.

RIGHT To avoid a visual jumble on open shelves, choose matching containers for foodstuffs (clear glass is pleasingly utilitarian in style, plus it avoids the need for labels), and use baskets to keep items such as napkins together tidily.

BELOW When you are in the middle of cooking, you don't want to have to rummage around in a distant drawer for a fish slice, spatula or wooden spoon. Keeping a collection of these things close to the stovetop in a container of some kind is a wise move.

be corralled – a ceramic egg tray could hold beads, while an old tin would keep tiny earrings together.

Textiles can play their part, too. Tote or drawstring bags, hung on hooks, can hold winter hats, gloves and scarves in the hallway or soft toys in a child's room, and zipped under-bed bags offer a breathable alternative to plastic boxes. Additionally, it's possible to buy fabric organizers that can be hung on a wall, over a door or from a clothes rail/rod – shelves, shoe-holders and pocket tidies are all worth considering.

Finally, spare a thought for how to create order in drawers and cupboards. Plastic drawer dividers can keep like with like in an underwear drawer in the bedroom, while large cupboards could become more organized with the addition of a small drawer unit or stacked storage boxes inside.

When it comes to repurposed storage, the possibilities are almost endless. Think outside the box, and you will start to see storage potential in even the most unlikely items.

OPPOSITE Old wooden drawers or storage boxes can be piled up and fixed together to create a sturdy, unusual shelf unit that's ideal for displaying quirky selections of objects. Make sure that their arrangement isn't top-heavy and, to be on the safe side, attach it firmly to the wall as well.

ABOVE LEFT When it comes to storing decorative possessions such as necklaces, hats and scarves, choose an option that also creates an eye-catching display. This antique glazed cabinet might have been meant for anything from taxidermy to china, but it works brilliantly as a showcase for a jewellery collection.

ABOVE RIGHT Waste not want not! Here, several old drawers have been given a new lease of life through their transformation into a bespoke chest. The fact that all the drawers are made in richly toned timbers and have circular drawer knobs gives the piece a feeling of coherence.

REPURPOSED

For individual and affordable storage solutions that don't skimp on style, you can't beat a bit of creative repurposing. Even if your DIY skills can only be described as basic, there are plenty of quick and easy ways to reuse containers, make shelves and recycle furniture to create unique pieces that look great and keep clutter under control.

Perhaps the easiest place to start is simply to use a container meant for one purpose for another – jugs/pitchers, mugs and jars are ideal for keeping make-up brushes tidy on a dressing table, or storing pens, paper-clips and rubber bands in the home office. Colourful silicone ice cube trays hold all sorts of little things, while tiered cake stands are brilliant for storing and displaying anything from jewellery to nail polish. With some basic crafting skills, you can also transform cereal boxes into magazine files (simply cut them into the right shape and cover with pretty paper), attach upside-down cup hooks to a chalkboard to keep chalk handy or create a jam/jelly

LEFT Turned on their side or end and fixed to the wall, old drawers can be a great alternative to wall-hung shelves. These examples have been lined with paper, to provide a backdrop for each little vignette.

ABOVE Vintage metal office furniture is a stylish storage choice – whether you opt for a piece with original paintwork or a stripped or polished finish.

OPPOSITE If you like the industrial look, check out hardware stores and salvage yards for the constituent parts of a unique shelving system. Scaffolding boards, metal plumbing pipework and pallets all work well.

jar rack for bits and bobs by using Jubilee clips to attach the jars to a length of reclaimed wood.

If you're confident using a drill, all sorts of wall-hung storage can be made by fixing other objects to the wall. Old printer's letterpress trays make an excellent display option for collectibles or other small items, and certain types of spice rack are great for using as children's book shelves. Books themselves can even be transformed into witty shelving; just choose sturdy hardbacks and affix support brackets underneath. Other great repurposed shelf choices include wire baskets, wooden magazine files (turned on their side, they are ideal slotted into a corner) and even salvaged industrial and agricultural items, from pigeonholes to chicken nesting boxes.

OPPOSITE Large storage pieces with commercial or institutional origins, such as shop fittings and display cabinets, can make a vintage-style statement in your kitchen. With a little adaptation, they could be repurposed as stunning island units, such as this beautiful mahogany example.

RIGHT From bakery units with slatted shelves to metal examples used in hospitals, there are many ex-industrial and ex-institutional trolleys available, which are perfect for use in lieu of a freestanding shelf unit (and they have the added benefit of being movable).

LEFT One of the most wonderful things about using repurposed pieces as storage items – or, as in this case of shelving made from bible rests, reclaimed materials to make new pieces – is their fabulous patina.

OPPOSITE If your home has grand proportions, museum cabinets are the best option when it comes to keeping and displaying possessions. This one offers extra capacity through the use of the space underneath.

With just a little lateral thinking, you can also create all sorts of racks, noticeboards and organizers. Fix a cork placemat inside a vintage picture frame for a unique noticeboard or jewellery display. Antique or vintage toast racks work just as well for sorting the mail, shower caddies have myriad uses (just hang from a hook rather than the shower), while a vintage rake head can act as a rack for anything from keys to kitchen utensils. Antique ladders can be leaned against a wall and used for towels or magazines, or hoist one overhead for an unusual take on a pot rack (simply add S hooks).

The possibilities are also almost endless when it comes to repurposing furniture, or creating floor-standing storage pieces from other items. Wooden crates and benches can be fixed together (and to the wall, for safety) to fashion a bookcase, vintage suitcases look great piled up to act as a side table, desks and cabinets can be transformed into bathroom vanities with some modification, and old doors can be recycled as anything from a coffee table to a hallstand. Of course, if all this sounds like a bit too much effort, simply choose furniture that doesn't require any upcycling to make the most of its storage potential – old wooden chests make perfect coffee tables, retro school lockers add a vintage vibe to hallways and filing cabinets are just the job for storing a treasured stash of craft fabric.

STORAGE BY PURPOSE

Ultimately, the best storage solutions are those which cater for their particular purpose most closely, which means the savvy way to tackle any storage challenge is to think carefully about what exactly is required from it. Are the objects small or large? Are they delicate? Should they be stowed away or kept on show? Do they need to be accessed regularly (read: quickly)? Once you know the answer to these questions, you'll be in a better position to choose how to store certain things.

If you lack the time to consider all of the above in detail, it makes sense to pick an off-the-shelf solution that's intentionally designed for a particular purpose, since in effect someone will have already done a lot of the thinking for you. However, with a little imagination and ingenuity, you should be able to figure out an (often more affordable) option that suits your needs perfectly.

The principles of clothes storage are that only clean items should be put away and that everything should be stored behind closed doors to prevent fading and to protect against dust and odours.

OPPOSITE Cupboards built into the eaves of a room represent the ultimate in understated interior style, as well as maximizing storage capacity. For a coherent aesthetic effect, these cupboards have doors made from the same tongue-and-groove panelling as the walls and ceiling.

ABOVE LEFT An ornately carved, French-style armoire makes a strong statement in this ultra-feminine bedroom. It provides an appropriate home for all sorts of female attire, from elegant dresses to chunky knitwear, and the mirrored front will prove very useful too.

ABOVE RIGHT Chests of drawers are best suited to clothing that is stored folded, such as sweaters, T-shirts and jeans, as well as underwear and accessories. Keep like with like (perhaps with the help of drawer dividers) and, if you're stacking things up, put heavier garments underneath lighter ones.

CLOTHES AND SHOES

It's said that we wear 20% of our clothes 80% of the time, so the first step to achieving a well-organized wardrobe is to conduct a clothing audit. Try everything on, and remove any garment that hasn't been worn in the last year, no longer fits, is uncomfortable or still needs mending (if you haven't done it yet, will you ever?). You might want to sell higher-value items through an online auction site, but if you don't think you'll find time, be bold and donate everything to charity instead. If there are clothes or linens you want to keep for sentimental reasons, or childrenswear intended for a younger sibling to grow into, store these separately.

LEFT **A pair of matching white wardrobes/armoires provides separate clothing storage for two people sharing a room. The space between them has been imaginatively used to display a few decorative possessions.**

BELOW **If you want to keep treasured or expensive garments free of dust and in tip-top condition, invest in specially made covers. Cotton examples are preferable, since these let the clothes 'breathe'; synthetic alternatives could leave your cherished clothing prone to mould and mildew.**

OPPOSITE **Never stack folded clothes right to the top (or indeed the edges) of a space, as good air flow is required to keep garments in the best possible condition. If you pack them in too tightly, you could be risking damage from mildew and the easy spread of moths and other pests.**

Clothes intended for long-term storage should be fully cleaned, wrapped in acid-free tissue, and placed in a clean suitcase, a storage box, or a space-saving vacuum storage bag. Don't keep clothes in unheated spaces such as cellars, garages and attics as you could find there's a problem with damp, which is detrimental to fabric. Once or twice a year, unpack everything, unfold the garments to check for signs of mildew or moths, then refold and repack them differently so that any creases don't develop into damage to the fabric.

Another way to streamline your storage needs is to separate your clothes into seasonal wear, and rotate them between the closet and a less accessible space. Guest-bedroom wardrobe/armoires and drawers are ideal for keeping out-of-season garments, while bulky items such as knitwear, winter coats and ski-wear are ideal candidates for under-bed storage.

The principles of clothes storage (which also apply to linens) are that only clean apparel should be put away, that almost everything should be stored behind closed doors to protect against dust and fading, and that the conditions should be right to avoid mildew and pests. Vacuum regularly to remove hair and dust (both magnets for moths and carpet beetles) and ensure that your closet is well-ventilated and not overfilled (air circulation wards off mildew). You might also like to add an extra layer of protection with mothballs, lavender or cedar to repel moths, and a crystal-based dehumidifier to avoid damp.

You'll need both hanging and flat storage, but let your clothes dictate how much you need of each. Shirts and blouses are best hung, and those in delicate fabrics should be matched with padded hangers. Shaped suit hangers will keep jackets looking their best, while skirts and trousers should be kept on hangers with clips (though trousers can also be draped over the rod of a wooden hanger). Knitted clothing should be folded, as it might distort when hung. Folding also suits casual clothing made from robust fabrics such as denim and corduroy. Try to fold everything in as uniform a way as possible (you can buy folding boards which help with this), and

OPPOSITE An economic way to create built-in closet space is to install a hanging rail in an alcove and simply put up a curtain (perhaps on a matching rail) to screen your clothing.

RIGHT Minimalist floor-to-ceiling closets are perhaps the best way to keep a bedroom or dressing room looking sleek and uncluttered, while providing plenty of dedicated space for clothes and shoes.

BELOW Tall shoe racks or cabinets are often a better choice than low designs if you have a lot of footwear, since they offer a much greater capacity for the same base area.

stack items loosely (to allow air to flow between them), with lighter garments on top of heavier ones.

As well as keeping clothes of the same season together, it's a good idea to arrange your garments by type and even colour, as this will help you find pieces and create outfits quickly and efficiently. By storing your most often worn clothes at eye-height in the easiest-to-access places, and always putting them away properly, you'll save even more time and effort.

Shoes and boots might be best kept in the hallway – close to where you'll put them on before you leave home – in which case consider investing in a custom-built cabinet or storage system to prevent them cluttering up the space and protect them from dust. If you prefer to keep your footwear in the bottom of the closet, then either invest in some racks or store shoes in clear plastic shoeboxes. An alternative is to take a snapshot of each pair and attach it to the exterior of their original box, helping you identify them at a glance.

Dividers, racks and rails can be used to make the most of both closet and shelf space. Although custom-built modular systems can be included when you buy new fitted closets, you can always take the budget option and fit out your existing fitted or freestanding cupboards yourself using bracket storage systems (or simply the odd extra rail or shelf). One easy way to increase hanging space is to fix a second hanging rail in a closet, as 'double hanging' will give you twice as much capacity – just make sure there's another hanging option for full-length items. In drawers, use containers or dividers to keep like with like.

Other ways of increasing capacity without buying new furniture include fixing hooks to the back of closet doors (perfect for smaller items such as scarves, belts or ties – or use a tie hanger on the rail), stacking storage boxes on top of freestanding wardrobes/ armoires, or hanging an over-the-door shoe holder (which can be just as useful for socks, underwear and accessories). It's also a good idea to have a small step handy to make sure you can easily reach higher shelves, and a hook somewhere so that you can hang the next day's outfit up, ready for a speedy start in the morning.

ABOVE LEFT Drawer dividers help to prevent accessories from getting muddled and entangled, and help to simplify your choice when deciding what to wear.

ABOVE CENTRE Hanging pieces of jewellery on a holder of some kind, rather than keeping them in a box, will prevent damage.

ABOVE RIGHT Here the otherwise unused space on the back of the door is home to a collection of necklaces.

OPPOSITE Display meets storage in this shoe cabinet – a repurposed bookcase. You just need to make sure that every single pair on show is completely gorgeous.

Nowadays we don't shop for food as frequently as we once did and we tend to buy in bulk. This has increased our need for effective and well-organized food-storage solutions.

OPPOSITE When deciding what should go where in your kitchen, think about which foodstuffs and china might be used together. For example, for a more efficient morning routine, it makes sense to keep breakfast things such as coffee pots and mugs, bowls, spreads and cereals close to each other.

ABOVE LEFT Some ingredients – especially exotic ones, if you're a cook with a global approach – have such stunning packaging that it would be a shame not to display them. Just make sure that the contents are not light-sensitive, and that the packets are either in frequent use or wiped regularly.

ABOVE RIGHT Herbs and spices, as well as beverages of various kinds, are ideal candidates for keeping on open shelves. The former are often needed at busy times (while you are in the middle of whipping up some culinary delight), while the latter are likely to be consumed daily, so easy access is important in both cases.

FOOD

Whatever the size of your kitchen, the same basic principles will always apply. You should store all foodstuffs – whether they be in your refrigerator, freezer or store cupboard – so that they remains in optimum condition for the maximum length of time, so that it's easy to see exactly what you have, and so that it's simple to reach items when they are required. It makes sense to arrange your food storage to suit your needs, so frequently used items are always at arm's length while more obscure ingredients can be tucked away in cupboards.

Start your food-storage organization with a big clear-out, throwing away all out-of-date items so that it's easier to see what your actual needs are (it's a good idea to repeat this process periodically). Then group your foods by type – typical categories might include cereals, lunches, tins, grains and pasta, baking, snacks, beverages, and condiments – and arrange your storage to suit your particular needs. For example, if you do a lot of baking,

then keep key ingredients such as flour and sugar close to the front of a shelf, while fine wines should be kept in the coolest, darkest spot in the kitchen (or, better still, invest in a wine fridge to ensure that optimum temperature and humidity are maintained).

Frequently used ingredients are best kept out on the worktop/countertop for ease of access – a loaf in a bread bin by the toaster; coffee and teabags by the electric kettle

ABOVE White goods are no longer always white. Refrigerators and freezers, in particular, are available in a choice of different colours and finishes.

LEFT Glass jars are great for seeing instantly what ingredients you have and what might need replenishing. For added freshness, choose designs with a rubber seal.

OPPOSITE These shallow open shelves make wonderful use of an unusually shaped room, and dry goods are kept within easy reach.

THIS PAGE In this white, minimalist, fitted kitchen, a run of mismatched vintage cabinets transforms a collection of ingredients into a striking design feature. Crucially, all three cabinets are painted in the same colour and all are of similar proportions.

ABOVE Containers with flat tops can be stacked up to make the most of your cupboard or shelf space. Be careful when using glass jars or bottles in this way; if you have young children, plastic alternatives are preferable.

RIGHT Magnetic spice pots can be attached to any ferrous material, so don't feel you have to use them only with the metal sheet they come with. They're good for storing other small things, too, such as cake decorations.

(in airtight containers, for freshness); and salt, pepper and oils close to the hob (when it comes to oil, choose a small bottle so that it's used up before it can go rancid, which will happen more quickly if it's not kept in a cool, dark place). Herbs and spices should also be kept near at hand but, unless you use them often, it might be best to stash them in a dark cupboard to maintain optimum flavour.

Organizers can help to keep cupboards, fridges and drawers in order – stepped display racks, bottle holders and pull-out caddies all help to maximize space and make it easier to find things. Keeping the fridge in order takes a little more consideration, since you need to avoid cross-contamination – use sealed containers, keep eggs in their boxes, and separate raw and cooked meats. Overstocking can lead to a greater risk of cross-contamination, so make sure your fridge is big enough for your needs. Similarly, the freezer should be kept well-ordered, and care should be taken to ensure that foods are well-wrapped, properly labelled and can't drip on anything else. As freezers run more efficiently when well stocked, it can be a good idea to fill any empty freezer space with loaves of bread, which are inexpensive, bulky and a good standby.

The number and type of books you have will help you to decide where and how to keep them. An assortment of shelves of different heights and depths will provide the most versatile solution.

OPPOSITE It's tricky to find a spot for huge tomes – though modern books are very rarely as large as the antiquarian examples seen here. These have been stacked on their side, on low shelves, in a traditional built-in bookcase, with smaller books positioned more conventionally on the higher shelves.

ABOVE LEFT If all you need by your bed is an alarm clock and some bedtime reading, why not stack books to create a platform for the clock in place of a traditional bedside table? If you choose similarly sized volumes for the stack, you can simply put the book you are reading on top and it won't look odd.

ABOVE RIGHT A quirky wall shelf apparently made from a book is ideal for a bibliophile's room – you can buy concealed brackets to attach to the wall, which allow you to mount a hardback invisibly and then stack other volumes on top of it. It's best to use colourful, chunky tomes with attractive spines.

BOOKS

If you only own a handful of books, the chances are that they will fit on a single shelf or make a neat pile under the coffee table, but if you have a more extensive collection storage may take a little more consideration. Before you begin, have a clear-out. Consider keeping only favourite novels and non-fiction works that you'll come back to again and again. 'Light entertainment' paperback fiction is a prime candidate for giving away, or you might even consider investing in an e-reader for this sort of literature.

Once you've weeded out any titles you feel don't deserve a permanent place in your library, then the number and type of books you have will help you to decide exactly where and how to keep them.

If you have piles of hardbacks, then you'll need to either place them on sturdy, low shelves or stack them on the floor (try piling them under tables, in redundant fireplaces, or even supporting a sheet of Perspex/plexiglass on top to create an unusual book-built coffee table). Collections of paperback fiction are more flexible, thanks to their lower weight and smaller size, so can be kept on narrower, higher shelves.

Whatever the make-up of your book collection in terms of size, bookcases with adjustable shelves are ideal, since you can space them just the right distance apart and therefore get the maximum number of shelves within the height of the piece.

ABOVE A low bench provides a home for a surprising number of books and magazines – its capacity has been maximized by stacking them rather than using the bench as a traditional bookshelf.

RIGHT A collection of glossy illustrated books is displayed on a multi-level coffee table – ready to be leafed through by curious visitors or pored over by their owner.

OPPOSITE Piles of hardbacks can even be used to support a table top made of wood or glass (or even an old drawer, such as this carefully balanced example) for a unique look.

John Currin
David Hockney Portraits
BILLY WILDER'S
SOME LIKE IT HOT
FAMILY
MODIGLIANI
IMPRESSIONISM
A HISTORY OF MODERN ART
EASY RIDERS RAGING BULLS
BRITISH HISTORY
ROALD DAHL
TOLKIEN
1001 MOVIES

Freestanding bookcases should always be fixed to the wall to avoid accidents – a case full of books weighs a ton and can inflict serious damage if it topples over. Similarly, if you plan to use wall-hung shelves, make sure the design (and the fixings you choose) can bear the weight – floating shelves, for example, are a bad choice for heavy books, whereas twin-slot rail-and-bracket systems will spread the load over a larger area.

Try to keep similarly sized books together, and then arrange them by topic – or perhaps by colour, if the aesthetic impact is important to you. Books can also be used as part of an attractive display on a mantelpiece or display unit. A good rule of thumb for such a display is to divide it into thirds: a third pictures or photos, a third ornamental accessories, and a third books that are either stacked, arranged in short rows, or leaning. Mix up the shapes, contrasting the sleek oblong shapes of the books with curvier elements, and try to make the collection look relaxed and not too perfect: think loosely balanced, rather than perfectly symmetrical.

OPPOSITE With two vertical arrangements of shelves and a single shelf across the top, storage for a veritable library of books has been squeezed into an awkward area of wall space around an opening.

ABOVE LEFT A book collection creates decorative impact in a hallway that's been painted in a single shade of grey; the vertical arrangement introduces a contemporary twist to a traditional-looking space.

ABOVE RIGHT Fitting perfectly into an alcove, this set of classic books with beautifully illustrated spines sets up a dramatic contrast between nostalgic charm and contemporary white-on-white interior style.

ABOVE LEFT AND RIGHT One way to encourage children to read is to place their books at an accessible height and arrange them in such a way that the covers can be properly seen, rather than with the spines alone on view.

BELOW RIGHT If even a whole wall of shelves is not enough to store all your books, some thoughtful design can help to provide more capacity. These rolling units effectively add double-depth shelf space without compromising access.

OPPOSITE If some of your books and files are kept on high shelves, it is a sensible idea to have a ladder available so that you can reach them safely – especially if they are needed (or wanted) fairly regularly.

For larger collections or home libraries, custom-built wall-hung shelves that stretch up to the ceiling are a must. When taking this approach, it's surprising how many tomes can be accommodated in a relatively small space. You'll need to keep a lightweight stepladder handy for reaching the top shelves when required.

Children's books require special consideration, since youngsters are far more likely to become keen readers if they have books close to hand and can dip into their story collection whenever they want. Shelves should ideally display the books front-facing, so attractive illustrations can be seen (try the Ikea Ribba picture ledges, or even repurpose an old plate rack), and they should be within easy reach, but it might be even more practical to have kids' picture books stacked in a box on the floor (or in a basket, an old play wagon or truck or a crate on casters). Position floor cushions nearby to create a cosy reading nook.

Effective toy storage will help you to restore order at the end of a busy day of play. The key is to divide and conquer — invest in multiple pieces that can hold a variety of different items.

OPPOSITE A traditional toy chest makes it easy for children to put toys away on their own (with a little encouragement) and the lid can be closed to keep the jumble of objects hidden, but an adult should supervise tidy-up time to make sure that the heavy lid doesn't come down too quickly on little fingers.

ABOVE LEFT In a pre-schoolers' play area, make sure that as many toys as possible are within the children's reach, so that they can choose for themselves without help. Soft-sided storage bags are a better choice than hard-sided containers; since their motor skills are still developing, children can be clumsy.

ABOVE RIGHT Old fruit crates make economical storage for toys and they cry out to be decorated with paint, covered with patterned paper, or adorned with stickers or ribbon. They are stackable, too. Check there are no loose staples or splinters that might hurt the hands of young children.

TOYS

If you've got children, then you'll know how fast their toys seem to multiply — and how much of a challenge it can be to persuade youngsters to tidy up at the end of playtime. Toy storage needs to be robust and to work hard — as it's accessed every single day it tends to see heavy use and is often pushed around or climbed on. Make everyone's life easier by sorting out a storage system that your kids can easily tackle, and it'll speed up the tidying process no end (as well as helping to maintain an aesthetic that's slightly less chaotic!).

LEFT **Play spaces beg to be decorated in a light-hearted manner and a riot of colour is always a good way to go. For a fun and funky take on open storage, paper each section of a shelf unit with a different colourful wallpaper and fill each slot with books and toys.**

ABOVE **An old crate has been upcycled to make a multifunctional item for the playroom. Its capacious compartment has plenty of room for toys and books, while the padded seat offers a place to sit and play or read – or the crate could be a toy in itself, as the casters make it the perfect ride-on alternative!**

OPPOSITE **Plastic crates are easy to wash, which is a definite advantage when young children are involved, as they are apt to wander around with sticky fingers or maybe a loaded paintbrush. These crates are stackable and can have casters attached to them for maximum mobility.**

From a play perspective, it's best to keep toys easily accessible on low shelves (make sure they are attached to the wall or are stable enough not to be pulled over when freestanding), and use baskets or boxes without lids to keep similar things together (building bricks, for example, or musical instruments). This will give your children maximum opportunity to choose and interact with their playthings. You could try labelling the containers to help them know what goes where, or, if they're too young to read, try attaching a photo instead.

In a room that's not only dedicated to play – be it a bedroom or a living space – you might choose storage that can conceal the toys from sight at times (to help your child get a peaceful night's sleep, or for an evening with friends after your little one's bedtime). Grid-like shelving units with storage boxes that fit inside will do this nicely, as do toy boxes and chests, but try to avoid putting everything into one large container or some toys will get lost at the bottom.

On a similarly practical note, don't just stack up boxes of games, or you'll find that they'll all need to be dragged out to reach one box. A baking-tin/pan rack turned sideways will provide 'shelves' for the boxes; this way, even pulling out the box at the bottom won't disturb the rest. Puzzles can be stored in this way too, although they will take up less room if you put them into individual zip pouches instead (clear pencil cases or heavy-duty ziplock bags work well), and include a photo of the jigsaw for reference.

When it comes to collections of toys, such as plush animals, little figures or toy cars, a solution that will allow them to be displayed – as much as keep them out of the way when not in use – will please your child immensely. A stack of clear-plastic shoe boxes is great for holding small dolls and their accessories; toy hammocks are just the job for teddies and their friends; and a low-level garment rail (try Ikea) or some decorative hooks on the wall will prove the perfect solution for a fancy-dress corner.

OPPOSITE White shelves against a white wall offer the perfect display space for treasured possessions. It's a sensible idea to keep delicate items on higher shelves, with lower shelves reserved for everyday toys and books.

BELOW LEFT Low-level storage furniture is a great choice in this attic bedroom, not only because of the dimensions of the space but also because it gives the child using the room easy access to possessions.

BELOW RIGHT A piece of storage furniture can even be transformed into a plaything. This shelf unit has been reimagined as a toy kitchen – which, rather appropriately, stores all the child's toy cookware and food.

Whether you're an avid scrapbooker, a keen cyclist or a dedicated cello-player, you'll need to find exactly the right home for all the essential equipment that goes with your hobby.

OPPOSITE In a barn studio, the challenge is to devise an organizational strategy that will let the creative juices flow unhindered. Big tables allow plenty of room for works-in-progress to be left out, while pigeonhole units keep art materials in their proper place.

ABOVE LEFT Plastic tubes, neatly stacked, can be used to keep all sorts of small supplies tidy, but they are especially well suited to holding button collections. Simply fix an appropriate button on each lid so that it is easy to see at a glance which design is inside.

ABOVE RIGHT When it comes to art and craft supplies, the 'divide and conquer' approach is the one to take. Storage units with lots of small drawers – card-file cabinets or industrial units once used for hardware and fittings, for example – are ideal for imposing order.

HOBBIES

Whatever your hobby, be it a creative pursuit, sport, practical skill or musical instrument, you'll need to factor in any equipment you own when you're planning your home's storage. You might be lucky enough to have a dedicated room for your chosen activity, but chances are you'll be more likely to enjoy it in a corner of a bedroom or living area, or be faced with finding somewhere to store bulky outdoor sports equipment such as skis or bicycles. Whichever is true for you, the general approach is still the same – choose storage to keep things accessible, in good condition, and possibly hidden from sight, too.

There are, of course, bulkier items you can't expect to hide from view if space is tight – for example, there's not really a way to hide a bike in a small city apartment. But there are some clever storage options open to you, including racks to mount them on the wall or hoists to attach them to the ceiling (these work just as well in a garage or outbuilding space, and are equally good choices for surf boards, canoes and car roof boxes). You can even find innovative shelf-unit designs that combine cycle storage with open shelving. If you have a small outside space, you can purchase specially sized sheds or even tents to keep bikes secure

LEFT If your hobby room includes a work station of some kind, it makes sense to keep frequently used tools and materials close by. In this room, a small shelf unit has been placed on top of the work table, so that haberdashery can be kept within easy reach of the sewing machine.

ABOVE AND OPPOSITE BELOW With a little creative thinking, all manner of things can be repurposed to suit the storage needs of your

hobby space – and the best news is that this can be done at minimal cost. Constituent parts of storage items can be bought cheaply at car boot/yard sales, in junk shops and thrift stores, or via online auctions. In this tidy crafter's corner, some old wooden crates, a plastic basket, vintage tins and a retro plastic food-scoop unit – which can be seen in more detail on the opposite page, below right – have been neatly combined to keep a crafter's stash of supplies in order.

ABOVE Rather than choosing one large cupboard, why not pile together a variety of different cabinet designs to produce a unique and flexible storage solution? The key to success is finding a common thread that connects all the disparate pieces. In this work room, they all have a quirky mid-20th-century feel, while the colour palette of muted olive, pale pink, turquoise and natural wood recalls a similar era.

OPPOSITE A bike is a difficult item to house indoors, but apartment-dwellers will be pleased to find that the number of specialist storage solutions has increased in recent years – from racks that attach to the wall to hoists that can be used to suspend cycles from the ceiling.

RIGHT If you have a lot of sportswear and equipment to store, why not consider changing-room style in the shape of a metal locker unit? There are several retro-style new designs available, or you could seek an original from a salvage yard or vintage furniture specialist.

and dry. For smaller sports equipment – such as balls, bats, sticks and golf clubs – you might find a wire basket attached to the wall, or a rack made from an old pallet, will keep things in order in the garage or shed, or if keeping them inside, perhaps it's time to invest in a retro locker or vintage storage chest.

Musical instruments can also be difficult to house, especially if you have several. Consider mounting guitars, violins, ukuleles and the like on the wall – up high, to free up as much space beneath them as possible. Larger pieces

such as pianos need floor space, so try to position them away from commonly used routes through rooms (or radiators, as extremes of temperature are damaging). If you're not displaying your instruments, then it's advisable to keep them in their cases; some might be best kept under the bed (buy risers if you need to boost its height a bit) or in an understairs cupboard. This approach also works for other hobby equipment that can be easily damaged, such as cameras and lenses, radio-controlled vehicles and optical instruments such as telescopes.

Hobbies such as jewellery making or woodwork that call for lots of small supplies and equipment require plenty of drawers and containers. Think about filling cupboards with mini drawer units or stacked boxes to keep things in order (clear plastic is best, so you can see what's inside), and don't forget the potential that your wall space has for storing often-used things within easy reach. Peg boards and slim shelving units are invaluable, and you could try attaching small baskets, boxes or shower caddies to the wall (or the back of the door) to hold bits and pieces, too.

Wall-hung shelves can be topped with containers or jars to hold little objects (you can even stick jar lids on the underneath of a shelf, so the jars hang below it, creating almost double the capacity). Filing cabinets come in very handy for storing bolts of fabric (draped over the hanging files); magnetic spice jars are ideal for tiny things like papercrafting notions or wood screws; while mug trees can make great stands for tools such as scissors and pliers.

ABOVE LEFT Keen gardeners know the value of keeping their sheds in order. A row of Shaker-style pegs or some large hooks will allow you to store tools and accessories well away from the floor.

ABOVE RIGHT If it's not possible to dedicate a whole room to your hobby, include plenty of storage within whichever space you plan to spend your leisure time. For example, this workbench has a cupboard that keeps tools hidden when they're not in use.

OPPOSITE A big noticeboard, and some wall-hung shelves, keeps inspirational things as well as tools and supplies close to the work station in this creative space, while larger items can be secreted in the sizeable drawer unit.

STORAGE BY STYLE

Your chosen aesthetic will, of course, be a guiding factor in your choice of storage solutions. While a consideration of what you have to store, where, and how often it's required is critical to both the practical and aesthetic merit of your home, the stylistic attributes of your storage will inevitably contribute to the overall decorative effect — and visual coherence is important.

You'll find that any chosen style will have certain storage solutions associated with it; retro living rooms might feature a sideboard or cocktail cabinet, while vintage-style kitchens often boast enamel canisters on open shelves, and a rustic-style living room could have a battered antique chest for a coffee table.

That said, there's no need to feel constrained to a purist approach, as it's usually possible to mix understated pieces with statement designs to boost storage provision without creating discordance. For example, plain shelves fitted into an alcove, simple cabinets (in a style-appropriate finish) and minimalist cabinetry are very versatile and can be neatly tweaked to suit any aesthetic.

A minimalist interior relies on clutter-free surfaces and floors. If you aren't naturally tidy, planning a generous amount of built-in storage is the easiest way to achieve this sleek, elegant look.

OPPOSITE Reflecting the utilitarian nature of this concrete-and-ply kitchen, sets of plain matching tableware are arranged in neat rows but, if desired, a sliding door can be closed to hide them.

ABOVE LEFT If you've got a room with unusual interior architecture, it's best to think minimalist and install cupboards with flat slab doors, so as not to detract from the interesting space.

ABOVE RIGHT A run of sleek white cupboards offers huge storage potential, and the curve helps to add a more fluid, organic touch to what might otherwise be a stark installation.

MINIMALIST

When it comes to storage solutions for the minimalist interior, the keyword is 'hidden' – the look relies upon all but a few very carefully chosen pieces being concealed behind closed doors. For this reason, the need to edit your belongings is even more critical than with other interior styles. Die-hard fans of the minimalist aesthetic might want to take a spartan approach, but that's not necessary if you plan your storage carefully. However, you still might want to consider measures such as whittling your clothes down to a capsule wardrobe, ditching kitchen equipment that never sees the light of day, switching from print to e-reader books, and choosing MP3 music and streamed video over CDs and DVDs.

Since your aim is clear surfaces and sleek lines, it's a good idea to over- rather than under-specify storage, both in terms of amount and quality. Custom-built storage is without a doubt the best choice, as it makes the most of every inch of space and can be designed with flat panels that either slide (doors) or push to open (drawers). Think handle-free cupboards or drawers under the stairs, a built-in cupboard that stretches the length of the living room (concealing TV and media players, amongst other things), beds with integrated storage beneath or even split-level rooms that boast drawers within steps and compartments underneath trap doors on the raised section.

LEFT The minimalist aesthetic demands that surfaces are kept clear of clutter. In the kitchen, this means devising sufficient storage provision for every ingredient, utensil, small appliance and piece of china and cookware. It also means that cleaning is made easier.

ABOVE For maximum efficiency during cooking, and for drawers that are just as beautiful on the inside as they are on the outside, every single item should be given its own place. Customized drawer inserts are essential for this approach.

OPPOSITE When everything is being stored out of sight, easy access is important. Deep drawers are a much more practical option than base unit cupboards, which make it difficult to reach items at the back – this usually involves kneeling on the floor and delving into the depths of the space.

When it comes to freestanding furniture, long and low proportions will maintain a contemporary aesthetic, while sleek lines are a must. Lacquer and fine timber veneer are popular finishes, always plain rather than patterned, and pieces in acrylic or glass (clear or mirrored) will avoid drawing the eye and keep the look understated – as will choosing furniture that's the same colour as the walls and/or floor.

Of course, there's no need to go the whole hog. Even if you don't want to create an entirely minimalist room, taking a similarly inspired approach can help you to streamline any interior scheme, and ensure it focuses on your favourite decorative elements.

OPPOSITE ABOVE A more traditional take on the minimalist look calls for fitted cupboards with some classic flourishes, such as understated moulding on the doors and contrasting knobs.

OPPOSITE BELOW A three-panel floor-to-ceiling sliding door wardrobe in blonde wood gives a sleek look to this contemporary minimalist bedroom – and the storage capacity inside is immense.

THIS PAGE A minimalist look does not depend on having fitted storage. Instead, you can choose handleless freestanding pieces with appropriate proportions for the space in question.

For country chic storage, stick to homespun, traditional pieces made from natural materials. Look out for homely pieces with simple lines and understated decoration.

OPPOSITE Open shelves, tongue-and-groove doors, painted finishes and cup handles are all key elements of a country chic kitchen. Here, an island unit provides storage in the form of several deep drawers, as well as plenty of preparation space, and delineates the cooking and dining areas of the room.

ABOVE LEFT Cabinet furniture with drawers made from woven willow enhances a rural aesthetic and can also be very practical. Vegetables and some fruit will benefit from being stored in a cool, dry place, rather than in the refrigerator (and the wicker allows adequate ventilation, too).

ABOVE RIGHT In a farmhouse kitchen, it is common to see rails or racks of pans and utensils hanging close to the range cooker. Here, a single open shelf also provides a convenient place to store a variety of decorative canisters and bowls, and provides a visual counterbalance to the angled flue.

COUNTRY CHIC

When it comes to finding suitable storage solutions for the country chic look, you'll find that there's plenty of choice out there. Whether you are shopping for antique, vintage, or new items, this style has a relaxed, forgiving aesthetic that is also perennially popular, so there's usually plenty of appropriate pieces available to buy.

LEFT This elegant kitchen features some essential ingredients of country style, such as painted furniture, natural timber and woven willow.

ABOVE Freestanding pieces add an authentic touch to a country interior. Here, a cupboard has been made to match the style of the fitted units.

OPPOSITE In-frame, Shaker-inspired cupboard doors on the base units hit just the right note, while leaving walls free of cabinets is another appropriate interpretation of country style.

Whether painted or waxed, wooden furniture is a key element of this style. Look out for homely pieces with simple lines and understated decoration – perhaps bun feet and tongue-and-groove detail – in natural timber tones or knocked-back natural shades such as cream, taupe and moss green. Provided you keep some kind of coherence in terms of scale, proportion, colour and (or)

detailing, you can easily mix a variety of country-style influences; an English stripped pine dresser can look perfectly at home next to a painted Swedish storage bench, while a wire-fronted French wall cabinet can certainly be teamed with an eastern European sideboard.

Open shelves are important for display purposes (this is a cosy, comfy look that can even border on the slightly

ABOVE Fitted Shaker-style cupboards painted in a neutral tone are the perfect elegant update to a country chic bedroom – just as they are in a country kitchen. This long run of cupboards offers huge storage capacity.

OPPOSITE LEFT Fine furniture can add a touch of glamour to a rustic room. Here, a cabinet with turned decorative detail offers a contrast to the tongue-and-groove panelled walls and natural fibre flooring.

OPPOSITE RIGHT Stripped pine is a characterful choice, with styles ranging from decorative carved armoires to plain unadorned closets. Reproduction designs are available, but nothing beats the character of an original.

cluttered and still get away with it), as are traditional storage ideas such as plate racks, butcher's blocks, corner display cabinets, dressers and bookcases.

That said, you'll still want to look at storage for concealing various bits and pieces. Stick to old-fashioned pieces made from natural materials. Baskets and vintage leather suitcases make great underbed storage boxes, while wooden blanket boxes can be used for their original purpose or as a capacious coffee table. Enamel canisters are a country kitchen classic, while drawstring bags hanging from a peg rail (or a wrought-iron hook) can hide all manner of things, whether in the kitchen, bedroom or bathroom. Top wardrobes/armoires with pretty storage boxes (or baskets, with a fabric liner to avoid snagging delicates), and use old fruit crates to corral books or magazines together. Traditionally shaped upholstered ottomans can offer capacious storage in a bedroom or living room – while doing double duty as seating – and antiques such as monk's benches can come in handy for stashing anything from shoes and boots to spare cushions.

Fans of retro styling will have plenty of choice when it comes to suitable storage. Track down original pieces via auctions, markets and dealers or invest in modern retro-inspired examples.

OPPOSITE Various wall-hung modular shelving systems, dating from the middle of the 20th century, are available from vintage furniture specialists, online auctions, car boot sales and junk shops.

ABOVE LEFT Upcycling mid-century furniture is a great way to create a retro look. Covering drawer and cupboard fronts with era-appropriate wallpaper is easy to do and adds a playful touch.

ABOVE RIGHT The retro look can be as subtle or as outrageous as you like. This Broyhill Mod Pop sideboard belongs in the latter category, featuring bright green injection-moulded plastic fascias.

RETRO

The post-war era saw an explosion in both clever, ground-breaking design and affordable homewares. Furniture with a specific purpose became available like never before, with items such as cocktail cabinets, kitchen larder units and dressing tables all coming to be strongly associated with the mid-century period. There's a variety of different looks that come under the umbrella of 'retro', from Scandi-inspired minimalism encompassed by cabinet furniture by Ercol or Nathan, to the futuristic 1960s vibe of plastic storage by Kartell and Vitra, via the American 1950s diner look with its pastel shades and chrome detailing.

Specialist dealers are the place to head for pieces by Modernist masters such as Eames, Wegner and Panton, while more affordable mass-market originals can be found on online auction sites, retro furniture retailers, antiques fairs, and, if you're lucky, charity shops and car boot/yard sales. If you're more interested in the look than authenticity, then you'll find a wealth of retro-inspired designs within the homewares ranges at both high street and online retailers.

If you need a serious amount of storage space, it's worth considering combining minimalist custom-built storage with retro freestanding pieces, as this approach will let the

ABOVE There are so many retro-influenced contemporary pieces on the market – including new examples of iconic designs – that you'll be spoilt for choice when it comes to finding suitable storage solutions for a retro-style room.

RIGHT Repurposed as a unit that offers potential for both hiding and displaying objects, this old **TV** cabinet is thoroughly appropriate for a retro room, as similar designs would have graced many a mid-century living space.

OPPOSITE The sleek mahogany sideboard (either actually designed by, or inspired by the work of, one of a group of eminent Scandinavian designers) is among the most iconic storage pieces associated with the 1960s and 1970s.

**OPPOSITE Post-war
furniture design was all
about creating pieces suited
to the modern way of living,
with the aim of appealing
to a new generation of
consumers. Lines were often
geometric, though many
pieces also featured the sort
of curves made possible by
new materials and methods
of manufacture. These retro
shelves are a case in point.**

**ABOVE Many designs from
the 1960s and 1970s share
characteristics with the
minimalist designs of today,
with high-gloss lacquer and
sleek long lines still finding
favour among design lovers.
It is frequently the colour
palette, and sometimes the
condition of the piece, that
gives away an original – this
shade of orange simply
screams 1970s.**

bulk of your storage provision blend into the background
and your favoured aesthetic come to the fore. For a more
eclectic approach, consider adding just a few retro pieces.
Ceramic canisters with geometric designs can add a flash
of colour to a white-on-white contemporary kitchen and
Ladderax shelving is a practical choice for a modern home
office, while a long, low mid-century sideboard/credenza
might be the perfect addition to a contemporary living
room. Another approach is to customize plain furniture
with some retro touches; perhaps a lick of paint in a
suitably nostalgic shade, or use fabric or wallpaper inserts
to dress up a plain bookcase or wardrobe.

Accessible and affordable, this nostalgic look is easily achieved if you are prepared to put in some time trawling junk stores, flea markets and antiques fairs.

OPPOSITE **Vintage style gives you plenty of scope when it comes to finding suitable storage solutions. Anything goes, to a certain extent, and there's no need to have deep pockets either, since tired and even fairly battered pieces of furniture can be granted a new lease of life with a coat of paint.**

ABOVE LEFT **Small items can be stored in vintage tins. It is worth taking time to create a harmonious collection. Choosing a particular colour scheme is the easiest way to do this, since all manner of different shapes and designs will look coherent together if there's a common thread in their colouring.**

ABOVE RIGHT **Look out for pieces that have potential. You can always repair and refinish something (or not, given that a little shabbiness is acceptable in a vintage-style room), or ask someone to restore it for you. This striking lime-green cabinet probably started life as a rather staid-looking brown example.**

VINTAGE

When it comes to planning storage, laid-back vintage style is one of the easiest looks. Not only is it a very practical option, but repurposing and customizing are an integral part of the aesthetic, and as the vintage look is perennially popular there is a multitude of style-appropriate solutions to be found in stores, flea markets or on online auction sites.

LEFT Vintage style doesn't always have to be about colourful painted furniture and pretty accents. This kitchen storage has a simpler aesthetic that goes well with modern minimalism, including mid-century-style panel doors (some of which slide open) and understated metal handles.

ABOVE In a vintage-style kitchen, old cupboards with imperfect finishes are perfectly acceptable. To improve their capacity and accessibility, make sure to customize them with extra shelves, boxes, racks and hooks.

OPPOSITE Three open shelves, edged with bunting and lined with a collection of china and utilitarian glass canisters, add a vintage edge to this classic kitchen – as do the mismatched chairs, which have been painted in a variety of 1950s-inspired shades.

Generally speaking, almost any modest piece from the 20th century can be deemed suitable, and there's a little crossover with retro too (though without the sleek Scandinavian influence of trendy designer pieces from the 1960s and '70s). Wooden furniture might be painted or waxed, while metal detailing or accessories have a patina rather than being highly polished. Mix in a little institutional chic (think along the lines of salvaged medical cabinets or post office pigeonholes), an industrial influence (hardware cabinets and factory trolleys), or even repurpose shop fittings and office furniture.

The vintage look can be achieved on a shoestring by hunting through online auctions, charity shops/thrift stores, flea markets and antiques fairs. It can take

time to find just the right piece, especially if you've got specific requirements in terms of dimensions. Look out for multiples of small storage solutions – three vintage canisters can look more put together than singles – and for any type of furniture with either a capacious storage space or lots of compartments. Chests and trunks, wall cabinets, old suitcases, tins and boxes, wicker baskets and hampers, and small display cabinets are all worth having on your shopping list.

Don't shy away from something just because it's a bit dusty, rusty, or needs some kind of a makeover – often all that's needed is a quick clean (shabby chic is all part of the vintage look), and if you're not keen on DIY refinishing then you could always find someone to restore it for you.

OPPOSITE AND ABOVE A mass of different glazed cabinet designs was produced in the mid-20th century, so, if you have collections to display, there is plenty of choice. However, you can always place fabric or paper inserts behind the glazing if you have clutter to conceal.

LEFT A stack of vintage suitcases can serve to keep all manner of things neatly out of sight – but remember that access is not as straightforward as with, say, a chest of drawers, so only those items that are not needed frequently should be stored in such a way.

When it comes to eclectic style storage there are no rules, but the most successful effects employ bold contrasts and play off different shapes, scales and colours.

OPPOSITE When it comes to creating an eclectic room scheme, it's best to limit your choices to a small number of distinct styles and perhaps a restricted colour scheme too, so that the finished space has some element of coherence.

ABOVE LEFT The beauty of this look is that you can build the scheme around storage furniture you already own. Here, an unassuming chest of drawers occupies the corner of a pretty vintage bedroom, but the presence of a mass of white-and-hot-pink feathers adds a contrasting touch of kitsch.

ABOVE RIGHT Eclectic interior design doesn't have to mean a space is packed with pieces with different influences. This pared-down example is a case in point, with a panelled period room boasting a table and chairs that both contrast with the interior architecture and with each other.

ECLECTIC

Since the eclectic look is characterized by the fact that it's not a particular style but is instead a glorious juxtaposition of many different styles, you might think that putting together an eclectic room scheme is straightforward. However, it can actually be more difficult to achieve an aesthetic that hangs together harmoniously.

LEFT **Although their styles are very different, this rustic wooden cabinet and industrial metal storage unit share some features that allow them to sit side by side harmoniously. As well as being the same height, they both have an aged patina and the designs feature horizontal and vertical straight lines as their only decoration.**

OPPOSITE **This large antique French dresser looks perfectly at home alongside a 1970s leather sofa and a set of modern metal-framed dining chairs. The secret of achieving coherence is to match pieces of similar proportions and use a limited colour scheme. In this room, putty, cream and other off-white shades are shot through with tan and orange, and accented with black.**

On the plus side, choosing an eclectic theme can open up your options when it comes to storage. As there's no requirement to stick to a particular period or style, you're free to select furniture that best meets your needs storage-wise. Want to install a clutter-busting minimalist kitchen in a high-ceilinged space adorned with ornate Georgian plasterwork? Go for it. Thinking of housing a book collection on sleek, white floor-to-ceiling shelves next to a 19th century chimneypiece? Great idea.

When selecting storage furniture for this type of look, it's wise to choose pieces that have some kind of coherence with the rest of the room. The proportions

OPPOSITE In this gloriously minimalist kitchen, all surfaces and shelves are cast from concrete. The visual interest comes from a colourful collection of cookware and utensils, with shots of bright orange, yellow and pink jostling for attention alongside flashes of red.

RIGHT Used as a room divider in an open-plan space, this understated grid-style shelf unit could be used in almost any modern scheme – though the proximity of industrial-style crates on casters, and accessories in wood and leather, results in a look that's quintessentially eclectic.

should be in keeping with the dimensions of the space and the scale of the other pieces (unless you're deliberately using an oversized element for dramatic effect), while echoing colours that are found elsewhere in the scheme will also help achieve harmony.

That said, it's also important to play up the contrasts – it's better to have pieces that are totally different in style beside each other, rather than the two being just subtly different (think how well a stark, contemporary sideboard looks in a parquet-floored panel-walled dining space, or how successful the stylistic interplay between an industrial metal shelving unit and the mellow brick interior of a loft apartment). Balance is key, too. Make sure your mix of styles is evenly distributed both through the room and through your home; this is easier if you choose no more than three styles to meld together.

A home that's more traditional in style lends itself to freestanding and custom-built storage that can both conceal more functional modern items and contribute to this elegant aesthetic.

OPPOSITE When choosing traditional freestanding furniture for a fireside alcove, be sure to get the dimensions right. A piece that's too small will appear mean and look out of place (as well as failing to offer maximum storage potential). One that's too big will make the space seem awkwardly cramped.

ABOVE LEFT An antique chest of drawers can give quite a formal air, but there are ways of softening the aesthetic. Don't feel you have to build a whole room around an authentic period style – mixing in a few more modern accessories will keep the look traditional, but lighten it somewhat.

ABOVE RIGHT Not only a great choice for a dedicated home office, an antique bureau can also be used in other parts of the home – perhaps as storage for a CD and DVD collection in the living room (providing a surface for your laptop, too), or as a place to keep household correspondence and family photographs.

TRADITIONAL

If you're looking to create a traditional look, then your storage provision needs to follow certain rules. You may have to try a little harder to find appropriate solutions, since some modern options aren't aesthetically appropriate. On a related note, one of the functions of storage in the traditional interior is to conceal from view any item that doesn't fit with the period look (so hiding modern tech is certainly a key consideration).

Freestanding furniture is generally the most appropriate for this aesthetic, whether it's a fine antique or simply antique-style, in a waxed, painted or French polished finish. Pieces can be plain or boast decorative detailing including carving, marquetry and turned detail; for coherence it's best to stick to one period style rather than mixing them up too much.

Carefully designed custom-built storage can be a great way to achieve a large amount of capacity – affluent Georgian and Victorian homes frequently featured cupboards in

LEFT Fitted kitchens are less than a century old, but that's not to say that they should be avoided if you want to create a traditional look in the hub of your home. Design features that evoke a suitably classic look include in-frame cupboard doors made from solid wood and featuring a painted finish, units decorated with moulding or perhaps those in Shaker style, glazed cabinets or open shelves on the walls, and a worktop/countertop in natural wood.

OPPOSITE This stunning room in a Georgian home looks authentic for the period – as authentic-looking as it gets without having to eschew the sort of modern conveniences that few of us would like to live without. A sink unit made in the style of a traditional freestanding table, open shelves with simple wooden brackets, a wooden drainer, and storage choices including wicker baskets and plain glass jars – all help to create a space that gets as close as possible to an aesthetic that recalls the property's historical origins.

alcoves and under the stairs, and built-in bookcases and kitchen dressers, so emulating these original features can not only add practicality but also an element of authenticity to a period home.

Reproduction pieces that bring additional functionality to classic designs are worth their weight in gold, for example upholstered ottomans with a storage compartment. Similarly, if you wish to maximize a kitchen or bathroom's storage potential with fitted furniture, there are plenty of ranges which feature carved decoration, glazed cabinets, ornate handles and knobs, and countertops with decorative edge profiles.

ABOVE LEFT AND RIGHT Whatever period style you prefer, you will find an extensive choice of pieces with useful drawers, from desks and bureaux to tallboys, chests and sideboards. Antiques of this kind are not only a good investment in terms of storage capacity but also maintain their value over the years.

OPPOSITE Whether it was placed in the dining room, kitchen or living room, the dresser/ hutch was once a highly valued article of storage furniture in many homes. From modest rustic pieces to grand ornate examples, the variations on a theme are so wide that you are sure to find something to suit your needs.

STOCKISTS AND SUPPLIERS

ONE-STOP

Crate & Barrel

From peg boards to storage cabinets, towel racks to glass canisters, this US store offers a wealth of storage options.
+1 630 369 4464
www.crateandbarrel.com

Dwell

All kinds of cupboards, cabinets and shelves in a contemporary minimalist style, with relatively affordable price tags, plus other types of storage solution.
+44 (0)845 675 9090
www.dwell.co.uk

Habitat

For affordable modern design with retro touches, this store is hard to beat. Plenty of choice in storage furniture, plus smaller storage solutions including boxes, baskets and trunks.
+44 (0)344 499 4686
www.habitat.co.uk

Home Depot

Storage solutions for the kitchen, laundry, craft room and garage are sold alongside wall-mounted shelving, freestanding furniture and closet organizers.
+1 800 466 3337
www.homedepot.com

IKEA

Famously affordable, functional Scandinavian design for every room – from storage furniture and fitted kitchens to stacking boxes and wall-hung hooks.
www.ikea.com

John Lewis

A British institution, offering quality freestanding furniture, kitchens, and other storage solutions. Never knowingly undersold.
+44 (0)345 604 9049
www.johnlewis.com

Pottery Barn

Wonderful selection of baskets, trays, boxes, wall shelves, organizers, hooks and racks, plus freestanding furniture.
+1 888 779 5176
www.potterybarn.com

Store

If it's a useful storage solution, chances are you'll find it here. A really useful resource for anyone sorting out their home's storage provision.
+44 (0)844 414 2885
www.aplaceforeverything.co.uk

The Conran Shop

Freestanding and wall-hung shelves, plus cabinet furniture and other storage options – including iconic designs such as the Penguin Donkey and Eames Hang It All.
+44 (0)844 848 4000
www.conranshop.co.uk

The Holding Company

Storage options galore from drawer dividers to wall-mounted modular systems – solutions for every room including bathroom, bedroom, kitchen, home office, hallway and living spaces.
+44 (0)20 8445 2888
www.theholdingcompany.co.uk

LIVING ROOM

Cox & Cox

Contemporary country storage furniture with a vintage edge, plus a few pieces with a more industrial vibe.
+44 (0)844 858 0744
www.coxandcox.co.uk

Graham & Green

Quirkily designed storage furniture, plus shelves, boxes, baskets and other containers. Perfect for eclectic interiors, and those with a vintage, retro or industrial-chic edge.
+44 (0)20 8987 3700
www.grahamandgreen.co.uk

Heal's

The place to go for designer contemporary and mid-century modern storage furniture, including famous pieces such as the Kartell Bookworm shelf and Vitra's Eames-designed ESU shelving units.
+44 (0)20 7896 7451
www.heals.co.uk

Laura Ashley

Classically stylish cabinet furniture, including media units and bookshelves, plus chests of drawers and sideboards. Also a selection of blanket boxes, some with upholstered tops.
+44 (0)3332 008 009
www.lauraashley.com

Leporello

Hand-crafted painted furniture with
French and Swedish style influences,
also offers a bespoke service for TV
cabinets and ottomans.
+44 (0)1483 284 109
www.leporello.co.uk

Ligne Roset

Designer furnishings for
contemporary living, great for
freestanding shelving and cabinetry in
a cutting-edge style.
+44 (0)1494 545 910
www.ligneroset.com

Oka

Beautiful range of freestanding
storage pieces with European and
Oriental style influences.
+44 (0)1235 433 930
www.okadirect.com

Roche Bobois

Achingly hip furniture for every room
of the home; the modular wall units
for living spaces merit particular
attention.
+44 (0)20 7317 8828
www.roche-bobois.com

The Old Cinema

Wonderful selection of antique,
vintage and retro storage furniture,
including some eye-catching upcycled
pieces.
+44 (0)20 8995 4166
www.theoldcinema.co.uk

BEDROOM

And So To Bed

Gorgeous handmade bedroom
furniture made in period and
contemporary styles, including chests
of drawers, wardrobes, dressing
tables and bedside cabinets.
+44 (0)808 144 4343
www.andsotobed.co.uk

Elfa

Wall-hung modular storage systems
that make the best use of built-in
wardrobes or dressing rooms.
www.elfa.com

Go Modern

Particularly good for its contemporary
Italian-designed bedroom furniture,
including a wealth of storage beds.
+44 (0)20 7731 9540
www.gomodern.co.uk

Sharps

Fitted furniture for the bedroom (or
home office), including sliding door
wardrobes featuring a customised
photographic image.
+44 (0)800 035 6426
www.sharps.co.uk

Sweetpea & Willow

A lovely selection of French and
Italian inspired furniture, including a
particularly good choice of trunks
and blanket boxes.
+44 (0)345 257 2627
www.sweetpeaandwillow.com

The French Bedroom Company

Beautiful French-style chests of
drawers, cabinets, armoires,
wardrobes, bedside tables and shelf
units – perfect for creating a
romantic boudoir look.
+44 (0)1444 415 430
www.frenchbedroomcompany.co.uk

The Storage Bed Company

Specialises in storage beds with a
mattress that lifts up to reveal a
capacious storage compartment –
options include side- or end-hinged
designs, or those with a lift mechanism.
+44 (0)20 8451 6999
www.thestoragebed.co.uk

KITCHEN

Chalon

Bespoke handmade kitchens in a
traditional style, as well as furniture
for bathrooms, bedrooms, studies,
libraries and dining rooms.
+44 (0)1458 254 600
www.chalon.com

Crown Imperial

Kitchens from painted farmhouse-
style units to minimalist designs, plus
fitted furniture for bedrooms and
living spaces.
+44 (0)1227 742 424
www.crown-imperial.co.uk

deVOL

Bespoke kitchens in Shaker and
Classic English styles, plus an unusual
retro-inspired design.
+44 (0)1509 261 000
www.devolkitchens.co.uk

Ella's Kitchen Company

Nordic-style cabinets for either the countertop or the wall, featuring retro food scoops for ingredient storage, plus spice bottles, bread boxes, hooks and shelves.
+44 (0)1588 673 976
www.ellaskitchencompany.com

Greengate

Cheerful vintage-style small storage including glass jars, enamel canisters and stoneware containers.
+45 39 960 333
www.greengate.dk

Lakeland

Invaluable source of storage solutions for around the home, with a particularly useful selection of kitchen organizers.
+44 (0)1539 488 100
www.lakeland.co.uk

Poggenpohl

Precision engineered contemporary designs from the oldest kitchen brand in the world.
+49 (0)5221 3810
www.poggenpohl.com

Second Nature Collection

More than 50 classic and contemporary kitchen ranges, including a variety of clever storage options such as pull-outs, larders and corner cupboard solutions.
+44 (0)1325 505 539
www.sncollection.co.uk

BATHROOM

CP Hart

Bathroom furniture in a variety of styles, from elegant pieces suitable for period rooms to cutting edge design.
+44 (0)845 873 1121
www.cphart.co.uk

Ideal Standard

Clutter-concealing bathroom furniture, including ranges specifically designed for compact spaces.
+44 (0)1482 346 461
www.ideal-standard.co.uk

Kohler

US manufacturer of bathroom vanity units in a variety of sizes and styles, designed with the luxury market in mind.
+1 800 456 4537
www.kohler.com

Porcelanosa

Modern, minimalist bathroom furniture as well as designs with more feminine, classic lines.
+34 901 100 201
www.porcelanosa.com

Roca

Contemporary bathroom furniture, with some designs featuring 'organizing boxes' to compartmentalize storage provision.
www.roca.com

Roper Rhodes

Fitted furniture at a range of affordable price points, including more traditional painted Shaker styles and trendy slab doors in a gloss finish.
+44 (0)1225 303 900
www.roperrhodes.co.uk

Scotts of Stow

From shower caddies to freestanding under-sink cabinets, this retailer offers a wealth of options for beefing up bathroom storage.
+44 (0)844 482 2800
www.scottsofstow.co.uk

DINING ROOM

Barker and Stonehouse

Sideboards and cabinets just perfect for dining room storage, in a range of styles from period reproduction to ultra-sleek lacquered minimalism.
+44 (0)333 920 8465
www.barkerandstonehouse.co.uk

Grange

Classic and more contemporary interpretations of French chic. This brand's elegant dining room furniture includes sideboards, dressers and display cabinets.
+33 (0)4 78 44 39 39
www.grange.fr

Made

If you're looking for contemporary storage for the dining room, this company's designers offer plenty of nifty solutions, including ultra-modern pieces and some with a retro twist.
+44 (0)344 257 1888
www.made.com

Marks & Spencer

Sideboards and dressers galore at this institution of the British high street. A choice of classic styles and edgier contemporary-looking pieces.
+44 (0)333 014 8000
www.marksandspencer.com

HALLWAY

Smart Storage Solutions

Push-to-open fitted drawer units for making the most of under-stairs spaces, as well as a similar solution for eaves storage in loft conversions.
+44 (0)203 468 8056
www.smartstoragesolutions.co.uk

The Cotswold Company

Lovely country-style hallway storage furniture, including shoe cabinets, benches, and coat racks.
+44 (0)333 200 1725
www.cotswoldco.com

The Dormy House

Brilliant for painted furniture in greys, off whites and creams, there's a wealth of hall storage options including cupboards, benches and shelves.
+44 (0)1264 365 808

HOME OFFICE

Hammonds

Fitted furniture for the home office, as well as kitchens and bedrooms, in a range of styles from classic to modern.
+44 (0)800 021 4360
www.hammonds-uk.com

Lassco

The place to go for ex-institutional and industrial shelving, bookcases and trollies, plus vintage shop fittings and office furniture.
+44 (0)20 7394 2100
www.lassco.co.uk

Muji

Particularly brilliant for its range of filing accessories and storage boxes, in acrylic and recycled materials, and shelving units in oak or steel.
www.muji.eu

Neville Johnson

Traditional and contemporary fitted furniture for home offices, plus also for bedrooms, living rooms, libraries and home cinemas.
+44 (0)161 873 8333
www.nevillejohnson.co.uk

Paperchase

Funky selection of box and magazine files, plus letter racks and in trays, amongst other small storage solutions.
www.paperchase.co.uk

CHILD'S ROOM

Great Little Trading Company

Large range of child-specific storage furniture, including play tables with integrated drawers and bins, and beds with drawers and cupboards.
+44 (0)344 848 6000
www.gltc.co.uk

Jojo Maman Bebe

As well as toy boxes and baskets for the play room and bedroom (and even the bathroom), there's a good range of bookcases and toy sorters which encourage children to select their own amusement.
+44 (0)871 423 5656
www.jojomamanbebe.co.uk

Notonthehighstreet.com

This small business selling platform is great for personalised toy chests, fabric storage bins, and children's storage furniture.
+44 (0)345 259 1359
www.notonthehighstreet.com

Stompa

Fantastic selection of storage beds and bedroom furniture, including both classic white designs and brighter, funkier options.
+44 (0)1943 608 775
www.stompa.com

Vertbaudet

Plenty of child-sized storage options, including toy bins, book caddies and shoe tidies.
+44 (0)844 842 0000
www.vertbaudet.co.uk

PICTURE CREDITS

KEY: *ph* = photographer; **a** = above; **b** = below; **r** = right; **l** = left; **c** = centre.

1 *ph* Jan Baldwin/architect William Smalley's London flat; **2** *ph* Rachel Whiting/The London home of interior journalist and blogger Jill McNair; **3l** *ph* Rachel Whiting/The home of Susanne Brandt and her family in Copenhagen; **3r** *ph* Rachel Whiting/Joy Cho, designer and blogger of ohjoy.blogs.com; **4** *ph* Rachel Whiting/Designed by Armando Elias and Hugo D'Enjoy of Craft Design; **5** *ph* Debi Treloar/ Lykkeoglykkeliten.blogspot.com; **6** *ph* Jan Baldwin/designer Helen Ellery's home in London; **8** *ph* Rachel Whiting/the London home of interior journalist and blogger Jill McNair; **9** *ph* Catherine Gratwicke/The home of Jonathan Sela and Megan Schoenbachler; **10–11** *ph* Rachel Whiting/Designed by Armando Elias and Hugo D'Enjoy of Craft Design; **12** *ph* Chris Tubbs/Ben Pentreath's flat in Bloomsbury; **13l** *ph* Rachel Whiting/The home of Jane Schouten of www.alltheluckintheworld.nl; **13r** *ph* Polly Wreford/Paul's beach house in East Sussex, location hire through www.beachstudios.co.uk; **14a** *ph* Debi Treloar/Nicky Philips' apartment in London; **14b** *ph* Catherine Gratwicke/Oliver Heath and Katie Weiner – sustainable architecture, interiors and jewellery design; **15** *ph* Chris Everard/François Muracciole's apartment in Paris; **16** *ph* Rachel Whiting/Karine Köng, founder and creative director of www.bodieandfou.com; **17a** *ph* Polly Wreford/New Cross location to hire through www.beachstudios.co.uk; **17b** *ph* Christopher Drake; **18l** *ph* Rachel Whiting/The home of Birgitte and Henrik Moller Kastrup in Denmark; **18–19** *ph* Andrew Wood/The London loft of Andrew Weaving, www.centuryd.com; **20** *ph* Earl Carter/The family home of Hanne Dalsgaard and Henrik Jeppesen in Zealand, Denmark; **21l** *ph* Debi Treloar/Mark and Sally Bailey, www.baileyshome.com; **21r** *ph* Polly Wreford/Paul's beach house in East Sussex, location hire through www.beachstudios.co.uk; **22al** *ph* Simon Brown; **22ar** *ph* Polly Wreford; **22b** *ph* Polly Wreford/The family home of Melanie Ireland, founder and creator of Simple Kids, Antwerp; **23** *ph* Debi Treloar/The home of James Russell and Hannah Plumb, the artists behind JAMESPLUMB, www.jamesplumb.co.uk; **24l** *ph* The London home of the designer Suzy Radcliffe; **24r** Rachel Whiting/The London home of the stylist and writer Sara Emslie; **25** *ph* Debi Treloar/The home of Virginie Denny, fashion designer, and Alfonso Vallès, painter; **26** *ph* Rachel Whiting/The home of the Ponsa-Hemmings family of xo-inmyroom.com; **27l** *ph* Simon Brown; **27r** *ph* Catherine Gratwicke/ The home of Yvonne Eijkenduijn of www.yvestown.com in Belgium; **28a** *ph* Rachel Whiting/The family home of Louise Kamman Riising, co-owner of heyhome.dk; **28b** *ph* Debi Treloar/The home of 'créatrice' and designer Stine Weirsoe Holm in Malmö; **29l** *ph* Simon Brown; **29r** *ph* Rachel Whiting/The family home of Camilla Ebdrup of luckyboysunday.dk; **30** *ph* Christopher Drake; **31** *ph* Debi Treloar/The guesthouse of the interior designer and artist Philippe Guilmin, Brussels; **32l** *ph* Debi Treloar/The home of photographer Nils Odier, stylist Sofia Odier and their two daughters Lou and Uma, Sweden; **32 r–33** *ph* Anna Williams/The Brooklyn loft of Alina Preciado, owner of lifestyle store dar gitane, www.dargitane.com; **34** *ph* Debi Treloar/Stella Willing, stylist/designer and owner of house in Amsterdam; **35l** *ph* Polly Wreford/Michaela Imperiali, www.MIKinteriors.com; **35r** *ph* Polly Wreford/The home of the designer Anne Geistdoerfer of double g architects in Paris; **36** *ph* Simon Brown; **37 l** *ph* Mark Scott; **37r** *ph* A house in Highbury, London designed by Dale Loth Architects; **38l** *ph* Paul Massey/ Michael Gianelli and Greg Sahno's home in East Hampton; **38r** *ph* Simon Brown/i gigi General Store; **39** *ph* Simon Brown; **40** *ph* Catherine Gratwicke/The home of Jonathan Sela and Megan Schoenbachler; **41l** *ph* Winfried Heinz/A Parisian apartment designed by Tino Zervudachi and Antoine de Sigy; **41r** *ph* Chris Everard/a house in Holland Park, London; **42l** *ph* Catherine Gratwicke/The cabin of Hanne Borge and her family in Norway; **42r** *ph* Polly Wreford/ The family home of Sacha Paisley in Sussex, designed by Arior Design; **43l** *ph* Andrew Wood/Howard and Liddie Harrison; **43r** *ph* Rachel Whiting/The home of Susanne Brandt and her family in Copenhagen; **44** *ph* Rachel Whiting/Niki Brantmark of My Scandinavian Home; **45l** *ph* Polly Wreford/ The home in Copenhagen of June and David; **45r** *ph* Polly Wreford/Stenhuset Antikhandel, shop, café and B&B in Stockamollan, Sweden; **46l** *ph* Rachel Whiting/Jonathan Lo; **46r** *ph* Rachel Whiting/the London home of interior journalist and blogger Jill McNair; **47al** *ph* Rachel Whiting/Karine Köng, founder and creative director of www.bodieandfou.com; **47ar** *ph* Debi Treloar/Debi Treloar.com; **47b** *ph* Rachel Whiting/The home of Sabine Engelenburg of engelpunt.com; **48** *ph* Debi Treloar, www.dearswallow.com; **49l** *ph* Rachel Whiting/The family home of Louise Kamman Riising, co-owner of hey-home.dk; **49r** *ph* Rachel Whiting/The family home of Louise and Garth Jennings in London; **50l** *ph* Catherine Gratwicke/The cabin of Hanne Borge and her family in Norway; **50r** *ph* Anna Williams/The home of the designer Josephine Ekström, owner of Lily & Oscar, in Sweden; **51** *ph* Debi Treloar/ The family home in Norfolk of Laura and Fred Ingrams of Arie & Ingrams Design; **52** *ph* Debi Treloar/The home of Vidar and Ingrid Aune Westrum; **53** *ph* Earl Carter/The summerhouse of Tine Kjeldesen of www.tinekhome.com in Denmark; **54** *ph* Debi Treloar/The home of Virginie Denny, fashion designer, and Alfonso Vallès, painter; **55l** *ph* Debi Treloar/Stella Willing, stylist/designer and owner of house in Amsterdam; **55r** *ph* Rachel Whiting/The home of Desiree of VosgesParis.com in Rhenen; **56l** *ph* Tom Leighton; **56r** *ph* Catherine Gratwicke/Tracy Wilkinson, www.twworkshop.com; **57** *ph* Debi Treloar/The home of Virginie Denny, fashion designer, and Alfonso Vallès, painter; **58** *ph* Jan Baldwin/Alison Hill and John Taylor's home in Greenwich; **59l** Rachel Whiting/Designed by Armando Elias and Hugo D'Enjoy of Craft Design; **59r** *ph* The London apartment of Adam Hills and Maria Speake, owners of Retrouvius; **60** *ph* Polly Wreford/The family home of Alison Smith in Brighton; **61l** *ph* Andrew Wood/The Paris apartment of Nicolas Hug; **61r** *ph* Debi Treloar; **62 & 63l** *ph* Rachel Whiting/The home of Susanne Brandt and her family in Copenhagen; **63r** *ph* Rachel Whiting/The family home of Louise Kamman Riising, co-owner of heyhome.dk; **64** *ph* Debi Treloar/Ben Johns and Deb Waterman Johns' house in Georgetown; **65** *ph* Rachel Whiting/The Berlin home of Nici Zinelli, designer of Noé & Zoë, and Knut Hake, film editor; **66** *ph* Debi Treloar/Family home, Bankside, London; **67al** *ph* Rachel Whiting/Anki Wijnen and Casper Boot, www.zilverblauw.nl and www.jahallo.nl; **67ar** *ph* Debi Treloar/a new-build home in Notting Hill designed by Seth Stein Architects; **67b** *ph* Lisa Cohen/The home of designer Marijke van Nunen; **68a** *ph* Debi Treloar/The home of Jeanette Lunde; **68b** *ph* Debi Treloar/Lykkeoglykkeliten.blogspot.com; **69** *ph* Debi Treloar/ Cristine Tholstrup Hermansen and Helge Drenck's house in Copenhagen; **70** *ph* Rachel Whiting/The home of Jane Schouten of www.alltheluckintheworld.nl; **72** *ph* Rachel Whiting/Fons and Katja Cohen, owners of imps&elfs; **73l** *ph* Debi Treloar/The home of designer Niki Jones in Glasgow's West End; **73r** *ph* Catherine Gratwicke/The family home of Clare Checkland and Ian Harding in Fife; **74** *ph* Polly Wreford/The family home in Denmark of Tine Kjeldsen and Jacob Fossum, owners of www.tinekhome.dk; **75** *ph* Rachel Whiting/The home of Britt, Jurgen and Mascha; **76** *ph* Polly Wreford/The home of Victoria and Stephen Fordham in London, designed by Sarah Delaney,; **77al** *ph* Simon Brown/Lucy Dickens; **77ar** *ph* Andrew Wood; **77br** *ph* Jan Baldwin; **78** *ph* Polly Wreford/A family home in Islington designed by Nicola Harding; **79l** *ph* Jan Baldwin/George Saumarez Smith's home in Winchester; **79r** *ph* Debi Treloar; **80l** *ph* Polly Wreford/a private house in Amsterdam owned by Ank de la Plume; **80r** *ph* Polly Wreford/Bruno and Michèle Viard, location-en-luberon.com; **81** *ph* Polly Wreford/The family home of Elisabeth and Scott Wotherspoon, owners of Wickle in Lewes, www.wickle.co.uk; **82** *ph* Debi Treloar/Architect Simon Colebrook's home in London; **83a** *ph* Andrew Wood; **83b** *ph* Chris Tubbs/artist Camilla d'Afflitto's home and studio in Tuscany, architect and interior decorator, Roberto Gerosa; **84** *ph* Anna Williams/The Brooklyn loft of Alina Preciado, owner of lifestyle store dar gitane, www.dargitane.com; **85l** *ph* Andrew Wood/An original Florida home restored by Andrew Weaving, www.centuryd.com; **85r** *ph* Polly Wreford/Judith Kramer, owner of webshop Juudt.com; **86l** *ph* Polly Wreford/The home in Denmark of Charlotte Gueniau of RICE; **86r** *ph* Debi Treloar/ www.flickr.com/photos/jasnajanekovic/; **87** *ph* Debi Treloar/ Cristine Tholstrup Hermansen and Helge

Drenck's house in Copenhagen; **88 l** *ph* Christopher Drake/a house in Salisbury designed by Helen Ellery; **88r** *ph* Debi Treloar/ Clare and David Mannix-Andrews' house, Hove, East Sussex; **89** *ph* Paul Massey/Hôtel Le Sénéchal, Ars en Ré, designed by Christophe Ducharme Architecte; **90** *ph* Dan Duchars/The home of the stylist Rose Hammick and architect Andrew Treverton in London; **91** *ph* Rachel Whiting/Designed by Stéphane Garotin and Pierre Emmanuel Martin of Maison Hand in Lyon; **92l** *ph* Andrew Wood/a house designed by Guy Stansfeld; **92r** *ph* Polly Wreford/Cathie Curran Architects; **93** *ph* Earl Carter/Robert Young, Robert Young Architecture & Interiors, www.ryarch.com; **94** Emma Mitchell and James Gardiner/www.mademoisellepoirot.com; **95l** *ph* Debi Treloar/The home of stylist Selina Lake, selinalake.blogspot.com; **95r** *ph* Catherine Gratwicke/The home of Martine Buurman, www.omstebeurt.nl; **96l** *ph* Rachel Whiting/The family home of Louise Kamman Riising, co-owner of hey-home.dk; **96r, 97-98** *ph* Emma Mitchell and James Gardiner/www.mademoisellepoirot.com; **99a** *ph* Debi Treloar/The home of Virginie Denny, fashion designer, and Alfonso Vallès, painter; **99b** *ph* Simon Brown; **100** *ph* Rachel Whiting/The family home of Camilla Ebdrup of luckyboysunday.dk; **101l** *ph* Catherine Gratwicke/ Oliver Heath and Katie Weiner – sustainable architecture, interiors and jewellery design; **101r** *ph* Debi Treloar; **102l** *ph* Catherine Gratwicke/ Oliver Heath and Katie Weiner – sustainable architecture, interiors and jewellery design; **102r** *ph* Polly Wreford/The Copenhagen home of designer Birgitte Raben Olrik of Raben Saloner; **103** *ph* Debi Treloar/The home of George Lamb in London, designed by Retrouvius; **104** *ph* Debi Treloar/The home of Guy and Natasha Hills in London, designed by Retrouvius; **105** *ph* Catherine Gratwicke/ The cabin of Hanne Borge and her family in Norway; **106** *ph* Debi Treloar/The home of George Lamb in London, designed by Retrouvius; **107** *ph* Rachel Whiting/The home of Ashlyn Gibson, writer, stylist and founder of children's concept store Olive Loves Alfie, www.ashlyngibson.co.uk; **108** *ph* Jan Baldwin/John Nicolson's house is available as a film and photographic location; **109** *ph* Catherine Gratwicke/The home of Hanne Borge in Norway; **111l** *ph* Claire Richardson; **111r** *ph* Catherine Gratwicke/The home of Hanne Borge in Norway; **112l** *ph* Jan Baldwin/Stylist Karen Harrison's house in East Sussex, available for photoshoots through Emma Davies (07734 617639); **112r & 113** *ph* Polly Wreford; **114** *ph* Rachel Whiting/Designed by Stéphane Garotin and Pierre Emmanuel Martin of Maison Hand in Lyon; **115a** *ph* Rachel Whiting/The Paris apartment of Thierry Dreano, designed by architect Sylvie Cahen; **115b** *ph* Polly Wreford/ The family home of Alison Smith in Brighton; **116l** *ph* Polly Wreford; **116c** *ph* Polly Wreford/ Judith Kramer, owner of webshop Juudt.com; **116r** Polly Wreford; **117** *ph* Simon Brown; **118** *ph* Debi Treloar/Mark Chalmers' apartment in Amsterdam. Kitchen custom-made by Pol's Potten; **119l** *ph* Polly Wreford/Clare Nash's house in London; **119r** *ph* Simon Brown; **120l** *ph* William Reavell; **12 r** *ph* Rachel Whiting/Anki Wijnen and Casper Boot, www.zilverblauw.nl and www.jahallo.nl; **121** *ph* Simon Brown/Lucy Dickens; **122** *ph* Polly Wreford/The London home of designer Suzy Radcliffe; **123l** *ph* Debi Treloar; **123r** *ph* Claire Richardson/The home of Jean-Louis Fages and Matthieu Ober in Nimes; **124** *ph* Simon Brown; **125l** *ph* Polly Wreford/Foster House designed by Dave Coote and Atlanta Bartlett, www.beachstudios.co.uk; ; **125r** *ph* Claire Richardson; **126l** *ph* Debi Treloar/The house of stylist Reini Smit in the Netherlands, reini@quicknet.nl; **126r** *ph* Polly Wreford/The family home of Melanie Ireland, founder and creator of Simple Kids, Antwerp; **127** *ph* Debi Treloar/The home and studio of the artist Nathalie Lété in Paris; **128** *ph* Rachel Whiting/The family home of Louise and Garth Jennings in London; **129l** *ph* Polly Wreford; **129r** *ph* Catherine Gratwicke; **130 al** *ph* Rachel Whiting/The family home of Louise and Garth Jennings in London; **130ar** *ph* Rachel Whiting/The family home of Rebecca Proctor in Cornwall, futurusticblog.com; **130br** *ph* Chris Everard/David Mullman's apartment in New York designed by Mullman Seidman Architects; **131** *ph* Polly Wreford; **132** *ph* Caroline Arber; **133l** *ph* Rachel Whiting/The Berlin home of Nici Zinelli, designer of Noé & Zoë, and Knut Hake, film editor; **133 r** *ph* Winfried Heinze/Elle and Aarrons' rooms, Riverbank, Hampton Court; **134l** *ph* Debi Treloar/ The family home of Shella Anderson, Tollesbury, UK; **134r** *ph* Claire Richardson; **135** *ph* Rachel Whiting/The home of the Ponsa-Hemmings family of xo-inmyroom.com; **136** *ph* Polly Wreford/Cathie Curran Architects; **137l** *ph* Rachel Whiting/Anki Wijnen and Casper Boot, www.zilverblauw.nl and www.jahallo.nl; **137r** *ph* Rachel Whiting/The family home of Paola Sells of www.sugarkids.es in Barcelona; **138** *ph* Jan Baldwin/The home and studios of the artists Freddie Robins and Ben Coode-Adams in Essex. Designed by Anthony Hudson of Hudson Architects, built by Ben Coode-Adams and Nick Spall (NS Restorations); **139l** *ph* Holly Jolliffe; **139 r** Rachel Whiting/The home of Jane Schouten of www.alltheluckintheworld.nl; **140l** *ph* Holly Jolliffe; **140r** *ph* Debi Treloar/Lykkeoglykkeliten.blogspot.com; **141a** *ph* Rachel Whiting/The home of Jane Schouten of www.alltheluckintheworld.nl; **141b** *ph* Debi Treloar/ Lykkeoglykkeliten.blogspot.com; **142** *ph* Debi Treloar/Designed by Sage Wimer Coombe Architects, New York; **143** *ph* Kristin Perers; **144l** *ph* Caroline Arber; **144r** *ph* Rachel Whiting/The home of Nadine Richter, designer and co-owner of Noé & Zoë in Berlin; **145** *ph* Debi Treloar/The home of the designer Myriam de Loor, owner of www.petitpan.com, in Paris; **146** *ph* Catherine Gratwicke/ The home of Yvonne Eijkenduijn of www.yvestown.com in Belgium; **148** *ph* Jan Baldwin/The home of Mary Martin and Carl Turner of Carl Turner Architects in London; **149l** *ph* Rachel Whiting/The Paris apartment of Thierry Dreano, designed by architect Sylvie Cahen; **149r** *ph* Dan Duchars/Architects Patrick Theis and Soraya Khan's home in London; **150l** *ph* Polly Wreford/Alex White; **150r** *ph* Jan Baldwin/The home of Mary Martin and Carl Turner of Carl Turner Architects in London; **151** *ph* Dan Duchars/Ian Hogarth of Hogarth Architects' home office in London; **152a** *ph* Jan Baldwin/the house of Wendy Jansen and Chris Van Eldik, owners of J.O.B. Interieur, in Wijk bij Duurstede, The Netherlands; **152b** *ph* Jan Baldwin/The home of Mary Martin and Carl Turner of Carl Turner Architects in London; **153** *ph* Polly Wreford/Cathie Curran Architects; **154** *ph* Polly Wreford/The family home of Alison Smith in Brighton; **155l** *ph* Tom Leighton/chair Katherine Pole; **155r** *ph* Jan Baldwin/ The family home of stylist Holly Keeling, www.hollykeeling.co.uk; **156l** *ph* Jan Baldwin/The Colemans' family home; **156r** *ph* Jan Baldwin/The home of photographer Joanna Vestey and Steve Brooks in Cornwall; **157** *ph* Jan Baldwin/The family home of Becca and Bill Collison in Sussex; **158** *ph* Jan Baldwin/Stylist Karen Harrison's house in East Sussex, available for photoshoots through Emma Davies (07734 617639); **159l** *ph* Simon Upton/Nancy Braithwaite Interiors; **159r** *ph* Polly Wreford/The home of Zoe Ellison, the owner of i gigi General Store in Hove, Sussex; **160** *ph* Rachel Whiting/The family home of Justina Blakeney in Los Angeles; **161l** *ph* Debi Treloar/The home of Vidar and Ingrid Aune Westrum; **161r** *ph* Andrew Wood/The home of Mark and Kristine Davis, Palm Springs; **162l** *ph* Andrew Wood; **162r** *ph* Rachel Whiting/ The home of Jane Schouten of www.alltheluckintheworld.nl; **163** *ph* Rachel Whiting/ Jonathan Lo; **164** *ph* Andrew Wood/The London home of Steven and Jane Collins, owner of Sixty 6 boutique; **165** *ph* Andrew Wood/David Richardson and Debbie Murphy; **166** *ph* Catherine Gratwicke/The home of Yvonne Eijkenduijn of www.yvestown.com in Belgium; **167l** *ph* Debi Treloar/Designer Susanne Rutzou's home in Copenhagen ; **167r** *ph* Debi Treloar/The home and studio of the artist Nathalie Lété in Paris; **168 l** *ph* Debi Treloar/The home of Jeanette Lunde; **168r** *ph* Debi Treloar/Arendal Keramik, www.arendal-ceramics.com; **169** *ph* Polly Wreford/The family home of Sarah and Mark Benton in Rye; **170** *ph* Debi Treloar/Dean Sawyer and Steve Drum; **171l** *ph* Chris Everard/Gentucca Bini's apartment in Milan; **171r** *ph* Debi Treloar/www.flickr.com/photos/jasnajanekovic/; **172** *ph* Catherine Gratwicke/The home of Nicky Grace of Vintage Fabric & Gorgeous Things, www.etsy.com/shop/NickyGrace; **173l** *ph* Debi Treloar/The home of Sarah O'Keefe, co-owner of 'The Cross' in West London; **173r** *ph* Debi Treloar/available for location hire at www.shootspaces.com; **174** *ph* Polly Wreford/The home in Provence of Carolyn Oswald; **175** *ph* Simon Brown/Lucy Dickens; **176** *ph* Katya de Grunwald/The home of Emma Wilson in Sidi Kaouki, available to rent through www.castlesinthesand.com; **177** *ph* Polly Wreford/Marina Coriasco; **178** *ph* Jan Baldwin/Ben Pentreath's Dorset house; **179l** *ph* Polly Wreford/London house by Sarah Delaney Design; **179r** *ph* Debi Treloar/Stella Willing, stylist/designer and owner of house in Amsterdam; **180** *ph* Jan Baldwin/Designer Helen Ellery's home in London; **181** *ph* Jan Baldwin/The Kent home of William Palin of SAVE Britain's Heritage; **182l** *ph* Jan Baldwin/The London home of William Palin of SAVE Britain's Heritage; **182r** *ph* Chris Tubbs; **183** *ph* Jan Baldwin/The London home of William Palin of SAVE Britain's Heritage;

INDEX

Page numbers in *italic* refer to the illustrations

ACKNOWLEDGMENTS

A huge thank you to Matt and Lucy for fending for themselves while I shut myself away for hours on end to write (though I think they both secretly enjoyed the opportunity to build more crazy Duplo creations and watch Studio Ghibli films). I'd also like to thank Paul Nash and his team for finishing our fantastic home office garage conversion just in time for me to write this book in it – the right working environment made such a difference.

Thank you also to Claire Chandler, with whom I discussed the concept for this book in its earliest stages, and who helped me pin down its structure. Of course, I am indebted to the wonderful team at Ryland Peters & Small. In particular I'd like to thank Annabel Morgan, who not only gave me the opportunity to bring this book idea to fruition but also guided me along the way, Christina Borsi, for her invaluable help with the picture research, and Paul Tilby, whose design brought together text and images to such stunning effect.